3

+12

D1582025

LEARNING. services

01209 722146

Duchy College Rosewarne
Learning Centre

This resource is to be returned on or before the last date
stamped below. To renew items please contact the Centre

Three Week Loan

2 8 APR 2007 RETURNED

- 5 JUN 2007 RETURNED

RETURNED

8 JAN 2008

1 3 JAN 2014

THE
TRANSPLANTED GARDENER

THE
TRANSPLANTED GARDENER

Charles Elliott

FRANCES LINCOLN

Frances Lincoln Limited
4 Torriano Mews
Torriano Avenue
London NW5 2RZ
www.franceslincoln.com

The Transplanted Gardener
Copyright © Charles Elliott 1995, 1996
The moral right of the author has been asserted.

The majority of these pieces have appeared previously in
Horticulture magazine.

First published in the USA by Lyons & Burford 1995
First published in the UK by Viking 1996
First Frances Lincoln edition 2004

A catalogue record for this book is available from the British Library.

ISBN 0 7112 2380 7

Set in 11.5/14pt Monotype Fournier
Typeset by Datix International Limited, Bungay, Suffolk
Printed and bound in Singapore by
Kyodo Printing Co.

2 4 6 8 9 7 5 3 1

For Carol, the real gardener

Every Man Now, be his fortune what it will, is to be *doing something at his Place,* as the fashionable phrase is, and you will hardly meet with any Body, who, after the first Compliments, does not inform you, that he is *in Mortar* and *moving of Earth,* the modest terms for Building and Gardening.

Common Sense, 1739

Contents

Introduction

The title of this book is, in one important way, misleading. I'm not really a gardener, not at least a gardener in the sense that I know a lot about plants and design and how to grow things. Of course, I've picked up a bit here and there, but basically I'm drawn to gardens for reasons other than personal expertise or talent. I enjoy working out of doors. I like to build things (and this includes digging large holes, a significant gardening activity). I am fascinated by the countryside and particularly its past; the feeling of having got an almost physical grip on vanished times through an understanding of the way things continue to be done as they have been for centuries is peculiarly satisfying to me.

What really interests me about gardening is the fact that as a form of human endeavour – I won't say art, though some would – it has created a world for itself. I delight in wandering around in this world. It exists in the dusty stacks of the London Library and the amiable peacefulness of the Royal Horticultural Society's Lindley Library, overlooking Vincent Square; it can be found in the splendours of Stourhead on a crisp winter day or the Chelsea Flower Show in spring or a tiny, crammed back garden in south London in high summer; it speaks in the stories told by a Welsh sheep farmer who knows a field where orchids grow or a plant hunter roaming the marches of Tibet. It is a world full of growing things and equally full of amazing characters – fraudsters, snobs, gentle obsessives, dreamers and authentic geniuses. Some of them will be found in this book.

In case any of the above gives the wrong impression, I should make plain that I am writing from the perspective of an American who transplanted himself ten years ago. I mention this not only to forestall any geographic confusion but also to explain something about another aspect of the pieces in this book.

Americans – Anglophile Americans like me, anyway – grow up harbouring a number of cherished illusions about what it's like over here. Village life, lots of history, country houses and a class structure straight out of the eighteenth century. It doesn't take long to disabuse us of most of these fantasies – but not quite all, and this is the extraordinary thing. There are parts of the British countryside that have unselfconsciously retained much of their beauty, their changeless ancient ways and their sense of the deep past. The Welsh Marches, where I garden now, is one of them. Such places should be treasured wherever they survive, and it is greatly to this country's credit that so many survive here: many more, I regret to say, than in America.

Some of the pieces in this book thus deal with pleasant anachronisms I've found in Britain and, in most cases, liked. Others simply try to figure out what the hell British gardeners are up to. Any transplant is bound to react with extra sensitivity to new surroundings, and I suppose I'm no exception. But I can still say with honesty that while I've sometimes been intimidated by English gardening expertise, which seems bred in the bone and far more taken for granted than among Americans, I've much more often been amused and pleased. I hope this comes through.

Writing these pieces – most of which appeared, sometimes in a different form, in the American magazine *Horticulture* – I've always been conscious of my status as a twofold outsider, as a foreigner and a non-expert. I'd like to think that this has its advantages as well as its drawbacks. While you won't find anything new and practical here about feeding clematis for bloom, you will, I hope, get a fresh sense of the oddity, wonder, age and scope of gardening as a human pastime and of Britain as the world's greatest potting shed.

FRESH GROUND

Rain

It is raining today. So what else is new? It rained yesterday too, and the day before that. And the day before that it really poured. In fact, the last time the sun shone was Friday, and today's Wednesday.

I don't mean to complain, but for anyone who wasn't born and brought up in English weather this aerial flood is a bit hard to take. If it isn't drizzle, it's a cloudburst; if it isn't a steady soaker, it's a gully-washer. Weather reports are reduced to distinguishing between rain (bad) and showers (good) to give us something to look forward to, as in 'Rain will be spreading from the west, followed by showers, heavy at times.' I hear this every morning at five to seven, except on days when steady rain is forecast. There may be some truth in the old gag that you can tell when it's summer in England because the rain is warm.

I used to welcome rain. When it's midsummer in the New England Berkshires, and you've got vegetables coming on, the problem is generally too little rain, not too much. I remember driving up from New York on Friday afternoons and looking eagerly for puddles because their presence suggested a local sprinkle or two had made life easier for the lettuces. It usually hadn't, which meant uncoiling the hose yet again and laying out the soaker. No need to go into the problems involved in getting water to the garden – the vegetable patch and the tap were on opposite sides of the road – except to say that I don't recommend trying to make use of culverts inhabited by woodchucks. At the time it seemed like a good idea.

Over here you tend to view rain in a larger context. I won't say it dominates human existence – that's going a bit far – but even those of us concerned about the welfare of growing things may have trouble keeping British weather in proportion. There is so much of it. No foreigner like me can hope to muster the degree of complacency shown by Dr Johnson when he observed, 'Rain is good for vegetables, and for the animals who eat those vegetables, and for the animals who eat those animals.' There speaks the True Briton. He's probably right about the vegetables.

In an attempt to get a handle on this matter, I've been studying rain charts. One thing I was stunned to discover is that my present garden, at Towerhill Cottage, near Skenfrith in the Welsh Marches, is located in something called a 'rain shadow'. Evidently the weather could be worse. A dozen miles or so west of us, further into Wales, is a hulking great bleak lump of high ground called the Black Mountains. What apparently happens is that the rain-laden storm clouds trundling out of the Atlantic and up the Bristol Channel (most weather systems tend to move in from the south-west) run into these mountains. Rising, and cooling as they rise, the clouds dump a good part of their liquid freight on the western slopes and the heights before coming down on the other side, where we are. Thus we are in the 'rain shadow' of the Black Mountains.

The consequence of this orographic phenomenon is that while we get, on average, 35 inches of rain a year at Skenfrith, the poor souls on the western side of the mountains get more than twice as much. On top of the mountains, rainfall can reach an annual average of more than 10 *feet*. These days, I'm happy to say, almost nothing but sheep lives up there, although tucked away in a valley are the ruins of Llanthony Abbey. The story goes that this establishment struggled along for several hundred years before being abandoned sometime in the fifteenth century. The abbot reportedly declared that he was tired of preaching to the wolves. Personally, I think that the rain got to him.

What baffles me is why 35 inches of rain a year seems so *wet*. New England gets an average of 43 inches of precipitation a year, according to the statistics available here. Since New England covers about a third more ground than Old England, and must have its own share of rain shadows and other climatic irregularities (Aroostook County is famously sodden, for example), this statistic probably ought to be regarded as imprecise. Still, aberrations aside, it's clear that there's not much difference between the two places so far as precipitation is concerned. Yet I never owned a pair of wellington boots until I came to Britain, and now I wouldn't think of going out to hoe the early potatoes without putting them on.

No doubt one reason for this perceived disparity is the difference in climate. It snows in New England, sometimes a lot. This is a blessing to the gardener because the cover does a wonderful job of protecting plants from wind damage and the upheavals of winter thaws. Moreover, snow feels dry.

It hardly ever snows in Skenfrith. The temperature hovers between 40 and 60 degrees Fahrenheit most of the year, occasionally soaring to 70 or 75 in the summer and plunging to around freezing on clear nights in winter. So when we get precipitation, we usually get rain. Definitely wet.

Another reason may be the kind of rain. (To a Londoner's ear this may sound a bit like British Rail's famous excuse for the collapse of commuter services under a light dusting of snow: it was, said a spokesman, the 'wrong kind' of snow.) A good deal of what we get is drizzle, something halfway between thick fog and actual rain – precipitation that accumulates slowly. Those splendid August drought-breakers familiar in the Berkshires, with plenty of thunder and lightning emerging from a livid violet sky, and a solid wall of rain marching quickstep over the hills and valleys – no sooner here than sluiced away – are regrettably uncommon. Of course, to a bush bean, which would much sooner have a chance to savour the rain, such an absence wouldn't be regrettable at all.

To make sense of the differences between drizzle and deluge, meteorologists speak of 'rain days' – days during which at least 0.01 inch of rain falls. We have a lot of rain days in Skenfrith, between 175 and 200 a year, on average. Some of them produce a great deal more than 0.01 inch, but when a fine mist is blowing in your face, changing the red clay under your boots into an especially adhesive form of mud, the actual amount seems less than important.

The British landscape glories in its abundance of rain days. I treasure the memory of a hillside meadow we once walked across in January sunlight. The grass, glistening with fresh rain, was greener than any grass I ever saw, the green of a Dufy painting or a glass of lime jelly. I never saw green like that in New England in any season, much less winter.

But even here, I've found, rain doesn't necessarily come when you want it to, or in the right quantities. After all, rainfall averages are just that – averages. During the last five or six years parts of Britain – especially the south-eastern corner of England – have suffered from drought, hard as that may be to believe. Rivers have dried up, water tables have sunk disastrously, and house foundations have started to crack as the underlying clay dries and shrinks. 'Hosepipe bans', which make the use of a hose illegal, have been a feature of every summer in and around London since 1989. So far there haven't been any hosepipe bans in Skenfrith, and I don't suppose there will be. We get our water through some makeshift pipes from a spring that is apparently never-failing, as if it tapped into an aquifer as big as the Ritz. If I truly needed to water anything, I could, and last summer, after an incredible twenty-six days without rain, I did haul out a perforated soaker hose and drench the vegetable garden, feeling feckless all the while. Perhaps if I'd been more scientific about it, keeping track of flow with rain gauges and such, it might have seemed less like bringing coals to Newcastle or baked beans to Boston.

According to a little book I've been reading called *Weatherwise Gardening*, even British gardeners should expect to do a certain amount of watering. To help us figure out exactly how much, the authors present a series of maps showing transpiration rates (that is, the amount of time it takes for a typical plant to take up an inch of water from the soil and give it off into the atmosphere) in different parts of the country at different times of the year. The point is that if a plant transpires an inch in, say, nine days in July, then you should measure the rainfall during those same nine days and make up the deficit by watering. They tell you how to do it on a weekly basis, offering a helpful table by which I discovered that my own spinach, potatoes and green beans expect to receive precisely 0.40 inch of water (human- or heaven-sent) per week in April, 0.65 in May, 0.80 in June and July, 0.65 in August and 0.30 in September.

All this makes splendid sense, like so many other complicated procedures I'll never get around to in the garden. (Double-digging is another one.) And it serves to remind those of us downcast by the damp that the British climate does afford the occasional dry spell. At the moment, though, it is winter, and from the window of my London office I can see dark clouds gathering yet again in the west. The weather report predicts more rain (not showers), and in the Black Mountains the rivers are overflowing. Yesterday alone 4 inches of rain fell up there, and the official word is that Wales has just completed its wettest November in twenty-two years.

So if it seems wet here to me, maybe it really is.

Shovels

Serious physical labour is not one of my favourite occupations, to say the least, but what with one thing and another I've been doing a lot of it lately. Practically every weekend last winter was devoted to moving large quantities (would you believe tons?) of earth, sand and crushed stone around the garden as part of a building project. This is heavy work. In fact, with any foresight I would have locked in a few muscular teenagers or engaged a man with a backhoe to take the brunt of it. The problem is that you can't get a backhoe in there any more, and while I did have a couple of boys for a short spell, they bowed out and went off to do something more congenial, like learning Urdu. As the possessor of a brutish rototiller, I'm somewhat spoiled in the shovel department, since I can usually avoid spading the vegetable patch, and as a rule my digging is mostly confined to transplanting and cleaning up after the moles.

About eighty years ago a man named Frederick Winslow Taylor, ME, Sc.D., approached the subject of shovelling scientifically. Taylor, who is known (though perhaps narrowly) as the Father of Scientific Management, professed to believe that 'every single act of every workman can be reduced to a science'. What this was to mean to the poor glassy-eyed assembly-line drone of the future who bore the weight of his theories doesn't bear thinking about, at least not here. But to me, waiting for my back to unkink after a day's over-exertion, Taylor's idea had a certain horrid fascination. Taylor conducted his investigations at the Bethlehem Steel Works, in Pittsburgh, where about 600 workmen were engaged full time in shovelling. Taylor's first task was utterly basic – to figure out the optimum load per shovelful. Too little and not enough got moved, too much and the worker couldn't keep up the pace. He concluded, after many trials involving 'two or three first-class shovellers', that by lifting exactly 21 pounds – not 18, not 24 – a man could move the maximum tonnage each day.

But a shovel that could hold 21 pounds of ore, say, was bound to be a lot smaller than one carrying 21 pounds of ashes, or of 'rice coal', which was light and slippery. Traditionally, a workman owned one shovel and used it for everything. Taylor immediately recognized that this wouldn't do and developed a range of different-sized shovels to be assigned to the workers according to the material shovelled. Then he made a few thousand time-and-motion studies with a stopwatch to pin down the most efficient way to hold a shovel, scoop a load (of earth, wood, metal) and pitch the load a distance. In the end he was prepared to institute some radical new working procedures.

The results of Taylor's innovations were not only impressive; they were – to an amateur like me – downright chilling. After three years of New Model shovelling, he reported, the plant had reduced the number of labourers required from 600 to 140. Where the average cost of handling a ton had previously been more than 7 cents, it dropped to 3.3 cents. And each man moved 59 tons a day, compared to the original 16!

Now, no amount of science is going to make me move 59 tons of anything in a day (or 16 tons, for that matter), but Taylor's observations about choosing the right shovel for the job hit close to home. While digging a raspberry bed in Ireland not long ago, I found myself conducting an experiment with two implements. (There were three to start with, but one proved to have a busted blade.) The first was a broad, flat shovel with a vaguely rounded nose and a short handle terminating in a 'T'. The other was a long, narrow Irish spade with the better part of a small tree for a handle. My aim was to excavate a 30-foot trench 10 inches deep, put in a layer of rotted chicken manure, stir it up, set out the raspberry plants and fill in around them.

It turned out that the shovel was virtually useless, being too wide and flat and blunt. The spade wasn't bad for digging, although it wouldn't pick up much; the blade must have been all of 15 inches long and 5 inches wide at the top, tapering to 3½ at the bottom. Terrific for cutting peat, as the Irish are wont to do, but a good deal less effective for clearing loose soil out of a trench. I did manage to finish the job, but my conclusion *à la* Taylor was that neither implement would win prizes for efficiency in planting raspberries.

Of course, none of this came as a great surprise. I knew exactly what I would have preferred to dig with – a standard American shovel. Any inhabitant of the United States would know what I'm talking about, but to be precise: the blade is shield-shaped, pointed, roughly 9 inches wide at the top and 12 inches long, with a flat tread at the top to put your foot on. It is also somewhat cupped and tilts forward slightly from the line of the wooden handle. The handle is long – about 4 feet – and shaped slightly to reduce weight and improve the grip. Okay? What could be simpler?

Simple it isn't. When I first came to England and went to buy a shovel, I naturally looked for one like my old favourite – a tough American standard with CONNECTICUT HIGHWAY

DEPARTMENT branded on its ash handle and a look of tired experience. I didn't expect a difficult hunt.

To my surprise, and eventual chagrin, I discovered that such a commonplace shovel doesn't exist here. I went to garden centres, I went to farm-supply shops, I collected catalogues and searched fruitlessly through the booths at the Chelsea Flower Show. What I found were spades in abundance, scoops you'd think of using for coal or snow, forks (spading forks and pitchforks of the lethal, long-tined sort they call 'sprongs' in Ireland), half-moon edging spades, even a bizarre device known as the 'Terrex Autospade', which through some mechanical wizardry turns over a spit of earth all by itself. Except for the sprongs, almost all the tools had short handles with a 'D' grip at the top; the edging spade had a 'T'. None had my fondly recalled pointed blade, much less a pointed blade and a long handle. And though I asked many times, nobody appeared to have any idea where in Britain I could find what I was looking for.

One day, in Hereford, I did come upon a shovel I thought would serve. It had a shield-shaped blade with a point, a forward tilt and a tread. The blade was a bit wider than I liked – perhaps 10½ inches – and the handle, unfortunately, was short, with a 'D' grip. And if 21 pounds, according to Frederick Winslow Taylor, was the optimum shovelful, this shovel spelled trouble. The whole thing, handle and all, was metal. It struck me at the time that weight might pose a problem, a suspicion confirmed as soon as I started using it. With a full load you could expect to be heaving better than 30 pounds. I still have this beast – it is totally indestructible – but apart from levering mahonia roots out of the ground it gets little use these days.

I now realize that my problem was in part a confusion of terminology. Rather than call a spade a spade, plenty of Americans, me included, call it a shovel. No Englishman would dig with a shovel. By preference, I wouldn't dig with anything else. And I also use a shovel to shovel with – say, loose dirt or gravel. In fact, my ideal tool is a shovel-spade. No wonder nobody knew what I was talking about.

In his wonderful *Illustrated History of Gardening*, Anthony Huxley points out that we really do have a cultural gap here. The long-handled shovel-spade goes back to antiquity. The Romans used it, and in the rest of Europe people still prefer long handles on their spades. But in the Middle Ages, for reasons that remain unclear (were they undersized?), the English turned more and more to short-handled, square-edged spades for digging, generally with 'T' grips. ('D' or 'Y' grips made from a forked stick, or – as today – with a wedged-open cleft handle, were a further British refinement, still more popular in the south than the north.) Only in a few out-of-the-way places in the West Country did the long-handled shovel-spade survive into recent times. Much derided, too: Huxley quotes the head gardener of Bicton, Devon, in 1843:

Their spade is an ugly, homemade, heart-shaped bit of heavy iron, with a great socket to it, and they form the handle themselves, by cutting a great heavy, lumbering stick out of a hedge, six or seven feet in length, about the size of a Kentish hop pole, so that they can always use it without bending their backs.

No one who has ever actually tried digging with an American standard shovel could have made that crack about 'without bending their backs', but it is the sort of thing I have become used to hearing from Englishmen. Huxley himself seemed to think that you rest the handle of a long-handled shovel-spade on your knee or thigh, 'which acts as a fulcrum while digging'. (Try it.)

I remain convinced that the advantages of the long-handled

shovel-spade are unarguable. The blade cuts readily into the earth, even hard earth; the long handle gives splendid leverage; and when you get the spit out of the ground you can either turn it over easily or pitch it some distance away. You can dig a blade-wide hole as much as 2½ feet deep (adequate for sinking a post) without having to paw loose dirt out with your hands, and cutting a circle around a shrub for transplanting is a cinch.

Having failed to find an American standard over here, I bought one (and a couple of extra handles) on a visit to the States and brought it with my baggage on the return flight. The check-in desk was admirably accommodating, if unbelieving. The next step is to convince some British manufacturer to make the blasted things. I have two scraps of evidence that suggest the shovels might sell here.

The first comes from the '100 Years Ago' column of the *Abergavenny Chronicle*: 'A correspondent to the *Chronicle* urged Monmouthshire County Council to provide longer-handled shovels for their road men in line with Cardiganshire and Carmarthenshire so that they did not have to stoop so much.'

The second, more up to date, is the fact that during the short time I did have the services of two boys – English to the core – they both preferred the American standard shovel-spade to any other available implement.

So if Kinsman and Langenbach can flog those fancy English hand-forged forks and spades to Anglophile Americans, isn't it about time Bulldog made a decent shovel?

PS. A year or so after writing the above I discovered that Bulldog had indeed started making a decent shovel, with a correctly shaped blade and a long handle. I got one. The handle, a straight, heavy pole, rather lacks sophistication (a trait inherited, perhaps, from that West Country blunderbuss of 150 years ago), but it will pass if you don't mind the weight. The blade is heroic – ⅛-inch-thick steel. The only problem is that the shovels remain very hard to find because they are mostly going for export – to America.

Giant Vegetables

Like most gardeners, I've inadvertently managed to grow quite a few giant vegetables in my time. It happens when a particularly shy zucchini hides under a leaf and in the space of a week or two takes on the dimensions of a medium-sized pig. At that point there is nothing for it but a smash-up on the compost heap and greater attention paid to picking the little ones before they get out of hand.

I have recently learned that there are two reasons why I should be less aggressive toward these monsters. The first is that in Britain people actually eat the things. They call them 'vegetable marrows' (the little ones, in distinction, are called 'courgettes', reflecting their un-English nature) and are inclined to serve them, the bigger the better, cut up, boiled and drowned in white sauce. If you find this hard to believe, I suggest you check with my neighbour Mrs Mitchley, who happily intercepts my compost-heap-bound specimens.

The other reason is, to me, more inspiring. If your rogue zucchini is big enough, it might win a prize!

You cannot go to a garden show almost anywhere over here without discovering that there is a whole class of expert garden-ers devoted to – indeed, obsessed by – deliberately growing giant vegetables. Not just zucchinis, either, but virtually everything from leeks to cabbages, from pumpkins to parsnips. As in our own county fairs, of course, there are prizes for beauty – the shapeliest radish or the straightest broad bean. But size seems to be the real challenge. It's almost as if the nation's gardeners are trying to make up for the fact that Great Britain isn't very great any more.

According to Margaret Robinson of W. Robinson and Sons Ltd, a firm in Lancashire that has been supplying special seed to competition gardeners since 1860 ('For vegetables that taste as good as they look – raiser and sole seed producer of the Mammoth Strain'), in the last decade or so tens of thousands of people have become devoted to growing giants. Once they have the bug, she says, there is apparently no stopping them, or their vegetables. Allotment associations, Women's Institute chapters, local gardening clubs and factory cooperatives sponsor hundreds of shows each year 'from the top of Scotland to the bottom of Cornwall'. Some specialize, like the Kelsae Onion Festival in Harrogate or the Appleby Pot Leek Club, while others cover the whole spectrum of edibles. As a result scarcely a year passes without new records being set. It's hard to keep up.

For example, only ten years ago a Mr W. Rodger of Crail in Scotland grew the biggest onion ever recorded. It was a splendid specimen weighting 7 pounds 11½ ounces. Today, the record is pushing 12 pounds (trimmed, mind you), and there's a £2,000 prize waiting for the gardener who can beat it with an onion grown from the Unwin Seed Company's new Exhibition seed. I have no doubt this will happen. In fact, the golden bulb is probably sprouting as I write.

One is tempted to ask what the gimmick is. After all, *my* leeks don't reach 11 pounds 10¾ ounces the way Vin Throup's do. I've never grown beets remotely like Norman Hosking's, which measure nearly 13 *feet* from top to tail. And Bernard Lavery's

17-pound radish is hardly conceivable in the purlieus of Tower-hill Cottage.

The answer is that there isn't any gimmick, unless you want to class patience, persistence and endless experimentation as a gimmick. Miss Robinson points out that there have been no abrupt increases in the level of competition, no mysterious new growth hormones or prepotent fertilizers, just better growing techniques. 'It's like when Roger Bannister ran the four-minute mile,' she says. 'People thought that was the last word in speed, but it wasn't. It's the same with the size of vegetables.' Asked about the secret of his leviathan onions, Yorkshireman Vin Throup replies simply: 'You gets your soil tested, and you adds what's missing.'

Nevertheless, raising competition giants does require *some* special effort. Let us consider the matter of growing a carrot capable of challenging the current champion, which is no less than 158¾ nches long. (This is, incidentally, an increase of more than 4 feet over the 1985 record holder.) I am indebted to Robinson for the following instructions. The essential element is a raised bed. Not an ordinary raised bed, either, but one offering your carrot a life of luxury.

Start at ground level. The autumn before sowing, dig over the earth to a depth of 1½ feet or so, incorporating a barrow-load of peat or leafmould into every 4 to 6 square yards. Then on top of this build a huge box out of boards – anywhere from 3 to 9 feet high, depending on your ambitions – filling it with a mixture of five parts soil, one part coarse sand and one part leafmould, plus a modicum of superphosphate and sulphate of potash. Leave the raised bed to settle during the winter, forking in a dressing of 4 ounces of calcified seaweed per square yard some time in February.

The next step is to make the holes. Shove a crowbar into the bed at 12-inch intervals. The holes should be at least 3 feet deep and 4 inches in diameter at the top; they will be filled with finely sieved potting compost, preferably well dried so that it runs all the way down into the bottom of the hole. Sowing should take place in late March or early April. Soak your seeds for three or four days first. Before planting them – an inch deep, three or four per hole – sprinkle Chlorophos (a branded insecticide powder) in each hole. When the seedlings are 2 inches high, choose the strongest and pull out the extras – *with great care*. Avoid carrot fly.

From here on, things get complicated and often a bit arcane. Basically, while waiting for the carrot to extend itself, you feed and water. Most growers have their own private formulas. Richard Hope, a swede specialist, crushes birth-control pills and adds them to the water. He figures that the oestrogen makes the vegetables take up more water. (Blackguard competitors aiming for weight have been known to *inject* water, or to insert slivers of lead into their onions or leeks. Some judges employ metal detectors.) Less adventurous gardeners rely on commercial fertilizers and supplements or on manure from a variety of animals, some bizarre. (A particularly effective, if odoriferous, tactic involves soaking the soiled bits of wool from sheep's bottoms – known as 'dags' – in a barrel of water and fertilizing with the resulting 'tea'.) Diseases and pests are kept at bay with chemical sprays, and for crops like leeks, in which perfect leaves are important, growing takes place under the shelter of plastic or glass.

Harvesting requires special care, particularly if – as in the case of your championship carrot – you are aiming for a long root. Remember that the greater part of the length will be a fragile – and inedible – thread. Fellow competitors prone to *Schadenfreude* relish the sad case of Alan Halman from Merseyside, who was washing a sure-winner beet one year when a 16-inch piece of root snapped off. Yet you can never be sure of what you've grown until you unearth it and get it cleaned up to show.

As competition gets hotter, more and more gardeners are trying to develop their own special strains of vegetables, but commercial seed companies still have the edge. Several, like Robinson, have spent years breeding the best for size. A surprising number of growers even prefer to buy their plants ready started. Miss Robinson notes that you have to be very dedicated to have your own heated greenhouse, and competition gardening is definitely not a rich man's sport. In fact, most of the biggest vegetables emerge from tiny backyards and allotments, where they are grown by retired men – almost never women.

The Olympics of monster-vegetable growing, the biggest of all in every sense (number of entries, size of leeks, etc.), is undoubtedly the United Kingdom Giant Vegetable Food and Flower Championships held each autumn in Weston, near Spalding, Lincolnshire. Now sponsored by the weekly *Garden News* and a slew of seed companies and garden suppliers, it draws growers from all over the country, who come toting their produce not in baskets but in horse trailers and moving vans. This is the place where records tend to fall. Last year Keith Foster of Whitby, North Yorkshire, took the Three-onion Class with a world-record 30-pound 7½-ounce combo. 'It's a tremendous feeling,' Foster was reported as saying. 'I grow leeks as well, but onions are the love of my life.'

Can you eat them? The assumption seems to be that you can't or wouldn't want to. 'It's bad enough having to cut them – that's the worst thing,' says Bernard Lavery, organizer of the Spalding contest and a grower of note. 'You look after them and nurture them – they're like kids, really.' Tom Anderson, whose

huge cabbage was 5 feet wide last July and still growing vigorously when he was interviewed at his allotment in Newcastle,
argued that consumption was impractical anyway. 'My poor wife
Evelyn would be blanching the same cabbage for the next twelve
months.' An editorial in the London *Times* sneered at the whole
phenomenon, claiming that giant vegetables are 'invariably dan-
gerous or poisonous'.

Miss Robinson, on the other hand, strongly disagrees. 'People
have a fetish about not eating giant vegetables, but they are
really very good.' I can't help wondering how you deal with a
pumpkin the size of a VW Beetle (five years of pies?), but I'm
not prepared to argue.

Speaking of pumpkins, it is necessary to report that they are
presently a sore point with the local giant-vegetable fraternity.
The British can be philosophical about the fact that the Japanese
have grown radishes weighing more than 70 pounds. They can
even live with American tomato records – how about a beef-
steak weighing 6 pounds plus? – because this climate simply
doesn't favour tomatoes. But giant pumpkins are something else.
They have a history here. What reader of P. G. Wodehouse,
that most English of novelists, can forget Blandings Castle and
the exploits of Lord Emsworth's monomaniac gardener Angus
McAllister, challenging nature and his fellow fanatics with huge
pumpkins destined for the Shropshire County Show?

Today, however, McAllister wouldn't stand a chance, nor, it
seems, do other British growers. The crown is firmly lodged in
North America. On only one occasion has the dismal pattern
been broken: in 1989, when a 710-pound pumpkin grown by our
friend Lavery held the record for three days before being out-
classed by a still bigger Canadian specimen. Since then, the
numbers in the New World have climbed inexorably – at last
notice a Californian held the record with an 824-pounder –

while, despite a standing £10,000 prize from a seed company, the British monsters are getting smaller. The biggest pumpkin anybody could lug to the Spalding show this year was only 413 pounds, practically a pygmy.

Wild Roses

There is said to be a wild rose growing in Hildesheim, in Germany, that is somewhat over 1,000 years old – a dog rose or briar rose (*Rosa canina*), the poet Rupert Brooke's 'English unofficial rose'. While the great age of this rose is interesting (if true), even more interesting to me is its fabulous behaviour. It seems that King Ludwig the Righteous, out hunting one day in AD 865 or thereabouts, misplaced a sacred relic. It turned up some days later under the rosebush. To Ludwig's chagrin – soon changed to awe – the rosebush refused to give up the relic. Heaven-struck, the king endowed a chapel forthwith.

To anyone familiar with the sort of wild rose now spreading across America, this tale rings true. A wild rosebush never gives up anything. I recall going fishing for trout in the Green River near Great Barrington one summer day a few years ago, when I still lived in the States. To reach a fresh pool I found it necessary to penetrate, or try to penetrate, a mass of blooming wild roses. Even if you are not carrying a fishing rod, this requires great concentration; an overlooked cane can literally scalp you. So I did not notice until much later that there was nothing but a few blood-flecked scratches left on the wrist where my watch had been. The bushes by this time looked all the same to me – huge white billows interrupted only by tiny crevices no intelligent deer would attempt to navigate except in an extremity. An hour's search failed to turn up the watch. My only consolation – and it was a small one – was the knowledge that the watch was battery-driven and would thus be ticking away there under the bushes for months, keeping time for the ants and the millipedes. Not the worst fate for a watch.

To an Englishman acquainted primarily with the briar rose – for the moment we will leave aside the cultivated varieties – such a confrontation probably seems unlikely. A briar can be an unfriendly thing, but isn't actually aggressive. It can be coaxed into forming part of a hedge, and its blossoms have frail, if transient, beauty. What must now be considered the classic *American* wild rose, the multiflora – officially *Rosa multiflora* – is something else again.

My introduction to this rose was a happy one, made the first springtime after we bought a house in the Massachusetts Berkshires. Mysterious plants were sprouting all over the place. A nondescript clump of reddish canes that had been drooping over the picket fence by the driveway suddenly leafed out with impressive vigour and almost immediately produced an abundance of unmistakably roseate blossoms. Shades of Old New England! – roses and a white picket fence.

What's more, it soon became apparent that these roses were authentically *colonial* – that is, they colonized. Smaller clumps began appearing elsewhere around the grounds. Gracefully flopping canes grew with no urging or care on my part. As a neophyte gardener, I was delighted. Of course, they were a little bit prickly. And somehow, once the blooms had passed, the bushes had a straggly, slightly arrogant, even hostile look that should have tipped me off to their true nature.

Now that I've left them behind, I can contemplate multiflora roses with equanimity (after all, there are 3,000 miles of safe distance between us). I know that they are not just 'a little bit prickly'; they can lacerate untanned elk skin. I know that their blossoms have about as much fragrance and visual appeal as a pile of white plastic bags. I know that only by chopping them down to the ground periodically and grubbing out their roots can they be kept from strangling everything in sight (including picket fences). Most of all, I know that multifloras are in a fair way of taking over the American countryside – certainly the Berkshires, probably most of New England and perhaps the entire United States. I base this statement on hard personal experience and on a fascinating article, 'A Literature Review of Management Practices for Multiflora Rose', by James E. Evans, published modestly, not to say obscurely, in the *Natural Areas Journal.*

The first thing I learned from Mr Evans's review of the scientific literature was that so far as America is concerned, multifloras are upstarts. They didn't even exist in the US until 1866, when they were imported from Japan to the East Coast to serve as rootstock for hybrid ornamental roses, having been brought to France six years earlier for the same purpose. It was a great time for rose breeding, and multifloras played their part with great efficiency. Today, in fact, it must be recognized that most modern floribunda roses are their descendants, and multiflora genes also contribute to the floriferous character of rambler strains.

Until the 1930s multiflora roses led a quiet and unobtrusive life, presumably largely underground. At that point, someone at the US Soil Conservation Service got the bright idea of using them to combat soil erosion and started giving away rooted cuttings. Cuttings were still being distributed in the late 1960s through soil-conservation departments in many parts of the country, though it is difficult to believe that nobody noticed what was going on. Because, in addition to functioning usefully as soil holders, hedges and crash barriers along divided highways (the latter being particularly appropriate, since nothing short of an armoured personnel carrier could make much headway through a growth of multiflora roses), the bushes were gradually spreading over meadows and unploughed farmland the length and breadth of the United States. Birds and rabbits enjoyed the shelter, but farmers noticed that cows wouldn't even enter a field full of roses, much less nibble on them. In fact, scientists running an experimental eradication programme in a New Jersey field found that cows were willing to eat the yellow plastic tape used to mark the rosebushes before they'd eat a bush.

Today, according to the evidence Evans turned up, multiflora roses are something close to a nuisance everywhere in the United States except those few areas where they do not thrive: the California and Nevada deserts, the south-eastern coastal plain and the Rocky Mountains. A number of distressed local governments have classified the plant as a noxious weed. Yet the spread continues, to the point where Americans may find themselves in the position of the New Zealand botanist observing the spread of an aggressive introduced variety of blackberry in his country a few years ago. On the west coast of South Island there was only one bush, he remarked, but that bush was 200 miles long.

Of course, there will always be a few people to speak on behalf of multifloras. Back in 1946 a soil-conservation man praised them as an ideal 'living fence', commenting inexplicably that 'seedling regeneration does occur under favourable conditions but not to the extent of constituting a nuisance'. He also remarked that the potential annual savings in barbed-wire steel would suffice to build a dozen battleships. Some sportsmen remain keen, defending the bushes for the cover they provide and for their 'aesthetic value'.

Aesthetics apart (and it's probably safer to leave them that way), most people who have had anything to do with multifloras in the wild these days consider them an irredeemable menace. No doubt they do indirectly conserve trout – I can testify from past experience that there are long stretches of streams in the Berkshires that are practically off-limits to anglers. A range of hideously prickly bushes 10 feet high, 20 feet deep and a quarter of a mile long may as well be the Great Wall of China. And they continue to spread, thanks to their habit of rooting wherever a shoot's tip touches the ground. Birds help, too; Evans delicately notes that seeds seem to germinate better after being scarified by passing through a bird's digestive tract.

So why doesn't somebody do something?

Well you might ask. The dismal fact is that in the wild rose nature has created a paragon of hardiness, a botanical dreadnought. (The Hildesheim rose survived bombing in World War II.) Repeated mowing works, but that's difficult to manage, given that the favourite multiflora habitats are along streams, on steep outcroppings or mixed into deep brush. You can try burning them, but experiments with a related wild rose in Texas (*Rosa bracteata*) demonstrated that fire isn't enough; regrowth started within two weeks and proceeded at the rate of 10 to 15 per cent a month. (A heavy dose of 2,4,5-T plus picloram, followed by more burning at intervals, did slow them down.) As you might expect, a bulldozer has been found to make a considerable dent in a phalanx of multifloras, but regeneration occurred faster than ever in the torn-up ground. Researchers have sprayed, sprinkled and poured a hair-raising variety of herbicides on wild roses with uncertain results. An impasse.

There's one other possibility, which I hesitate to mention for fear of raising hopes. A tiny, seed-eating wasp, the European rose chalcid (*Megastigmus aculeatus*), is particularly fond of wild-rose seeds. The female wasp (and most of them are female) deposits one egg inside a still forming seed. The larva develops and consumes the entire contents of the seed, rendering it sterile, and later emerges full-grown and ready to inject another seed. With enough wasps this could – theoretically – slow down, if not doom, *Rosa multiflora*. But, as usual, there's a catch. *Megastigmus aculeatus* don't fly much. You might say that they are exceptionally languid creatures. It may be necessary to carry them from bush to bush. I can't quite see anybody doing that.

It strikes me that, so far as multiflora roses are concerned, we are in an enviable position on this side of the Atlantic. The rootstock still comes in handy – according to the gardening writer Christopher Lloyd, it is exceptionally resistant to the dread Rose Sickness, a mysterious disease affecting new bushes planted in ground where roses have been grown before. But we have so far been spared the complete plant ramping through the wild, although a few nurseries stock it. I, for one, am grateful. After all, even a 'Kiftsgate' rose won't migrate next door.

In these circumstances I hope it will not be taken as presumptuous of me to make a suggestion to my former countrymen. When it comes to wild roses, the best idea of all may be King Ludwig's: build a chapel and pray.

Privacy

There is a gap in the hedge along our lane. It isn't very big —
maybe 2 or 3 feet, diminished a bit more by a bramble or two
and a fragment of privet. But it's big enough to see through. In
fact, people walking along the lane (and quite a few do, possibly
four a day on a nice weekend, because we are on a favourite
ramblers' route between castles) can gape through the gap and —
horrors — *see us*.

To be honest, I don't feel strongly about this. My companion
Carol is the one who does. Like most Britons (she's actually
Irish, but typically English in this one respect), she is unsettled
by gaps in hedges, fences with boards missing, enclosures that
fail to enclose. It's a matter of privacy. An Englishman's home
may be his castle, but his garden is definitely inside the wall.
Strangers peer in at their peril.

Plainly, there's a cultural gap here a good deal bigger than
that gap in the hedge (which, I assure you, will be filled soon).
Driving through New England last autumn on a visit, I was
struck by the oddness of something I had always taken for
granted before: the way Americans deliberately avoid shutting
themselves and their property in. While you may see a low
hedge or shrub bed marking the boundary of someone's house
lot, you don't see too many high fences; more likely the drive-

way will be doing the job. Picket fences hardly count – what could be less excluding visually than a white picket fence? – and the small-town and rural ideal seems to be expanses of open lawn, trees and some foundation plantings around the house. One yard runs right into the next. If you want to see what your neighbour is having for breakfast and you've got binoculars, no problem.

As an American, I'm perfectly comfortable with openness. It may be boring, but I grew up with it and can't get exercised about the lack of privacy it entails. Our national attitude probably has something to do with the pioneer abhorrence of trees and darkness; until they reached the Great Plains our ancestors' greatest ambition was to lay waste to enough forest to be able to see the sun and plant corn and potatoes. Fences and walls were strictly secondary and, in any case, meant for animals. In the same way, building pioneer villages on New England hilltops, instead of in valleys, probably had as much to do with wanting sunlight as with avoiding swamps. But such exposure is anathema to the Englishman.

You can see it in the tight little gardens jammed behind virtually every terraced house in London – 15 by 20 feet (modest), 25 by 70 feet (grand) – bounded by larch-board fencing topped by trellis. You can see it in the laurels and rhododendrons hiding the villas of the stockbroker belt. You can see it in the solid 7-foot hedges of privet or hawthorn or yew surrounding more modest properties in the suburbs. Inside these botanical barricades the English gardener goes his private way, comfortable in the knowledge that his neighbours can't see him, he can't see them, and the entire world – or what he's got of it – is green.

He is not, by the way, working in his 'yard'. While we are on the subject of significant differences, this is one that probably deserves mention. I now know that in Britain (and Ireland too), the word 'yard' refers only to a utilitarian area enclosed by a house and its outbuildings – the stables, say, if the house boasts such a thing. It's usually paved. The rest of the surroundings – lawns, shrub and flowerbeds, even the hedges, for that matter – are the 'garden'. So when an Englishman talks about his garden, he's talking about the whole works, not just the parts of it where cabbages and petunias are growing. This can be confusing to Americans and vice versa.

The British compulsion to fortify the garden has led to serious thought about the best way to do it. In city back gardens, the wooden fence seems to be most favoured (there isn't room for anything else, and it has the virtue of opacity). Brick walls are lovely, especially when they are 200 or 300 years old, but not particularly common as garden boundaries except in true brick country like Kent; on the grounds of country estates you are more likely to find brick used to enclose kitchen gardens and the like. Basically, hedges are the thing.

Those of us who garden in the countryside probably already have hedges, orginally planted to keep animals either in or out. Towerhill Cottage has plenty of them, not only the gappy one protecting us from traffic on the lane but others in various stages of dissolution along the edge of the wood and elsewhere. (By 'dissolution' I mean achieving their natural destiny as rows of trees knitted together with brush and brambles. This happens automatically within about ten years if you don't keep them sheared.) We have even planted a new hedge, a 20-foot stretch of *Lonicera nitida* that will form a boundary between the orchard and the lawn and is already 2 feet high after only eighteen months. I find it hard to believe that this plant is really a honeysuckle, because it does make a nice crisp evergreen hedge, provided you go over it five or six times a year with clippers. And you can't see through it.

Gardening books here are full of advice about hedges – what plants to use and how to train them. I'm rather more concerned about keeping the extremely miscellaneous hedges we've got under control. After all, we're talking about a mixture of holly, privet, elder, ash, hawthorn and even a rather handsome chunk of yew. But if you are really desperate to shut yourself in, one solution that I've never seen in a gardening book turned up in an article in the London *Times* last year. It seems that a landscape contractor in Devon has worked out a way to transplant an entire living hedge, leaf litter, primroses, rabbits and all, using a mechanical digger. Keith Banyard figures he can move an existing hedge for £5 a metre (a third the cost of planting a new hedge, fencing it against predators and tending it for the requisite two years of infancy).

It's conceivable that Banyard's invention could revolutionize the hedge-growing business. Talk about Birnam Wood coming to Dunsinane! Here's instant privacy for five quid a metre, and all green, too. But we have to ask whether it's likely to do anything at all to reduce the sort of conflicts that this British tight-little-island mentality is always giving rise to. Who, for instance, owns the hedge when it's on the property line? Whose responsibility is it to put up a new fence when the old one collapses under its load of *Clematis montana*? What about that next-door laburnum drooping its (poisonous) yellow chains over the children's sand-pit? And what about the hedge that grows too *big*?

In its pragmatic way, English common law has gradually over the centuries established ways of settling matters like these by precedent, rather in the way it has developed laws to deal with salmon poachers (they are no longer actually hanged). Your deed may well specify exactly who owns the fence, for instance (and if you are uncertain, you can tell by which side the posts are on). You may legally pick the apples from a neighbour's tree if the branch overhangs your garden. Still, such matters frequently end up in court. Newspaper readers have been greatly entertained here lately, for example, by the saga of Mr Stanton's hedge.

In 1971 Charles Stanton planted a row of small Leyland cypress (× *Cupressocyparis leylandii*) along the boundary fence between his garden and that of Michael Jones in Selly Oak, a suburb of Birmingham. 'I didn't notice because they were tiny little things,' says Jones, a retired teacher. By 1975 the trees had grown to about 10 feet. 'In drought summers we were watering them for him and keeping them alive. They looked like a fairytale picture. Bloody fools we were.'

As Jones described it — in court — the trees had grown to 35 feet by 1979: 'They were an immense nuisance.' For one thing, the Joneses' house was only 35 feet from the fence line, and winter gales threatened to topple the monsters. For another, the hedge completely excluded sunlight from the garden where the Joneses had been growing prize-winning fuchsias, lobelias and (dwarf) conifers. Stanton, a retired engineer, agreed to prune the trees to 25 feet.

But they grew back, as *leylandii* will. In 1989, depressed and presumably wan from lack of sunlight, Jones took matters into his own hands, removing what he claims was about 5 feet from the top of the hedge. 'I had to do them gradually,' he reported, 'because I'm elderly, arthritic, fat and, for that matter, bald. When I took one off there was great rage.' Stanton called the police.

From here on, everything but the *leylandii* went downhill. Stanton sprayed Jones with a hose. Jones responded by more dawn raids on the trees. Stanton's son was arrested after a violent encounter with Jones. Stanton sued Jones for trespass. The hedge grew on.

Last autumn, following a series of court hearings, an appeal court ruled against Stanton, declaring that the trees constituted a party hedge and Jones was within his rights to attack them. Lady Justice Butler-Sloss went so far as to comment that Jones had 'a very nice garden' before pleading with the two men to resolve their differences. Otherwise one or both of them might be bankrupted – court costs were already about £50,000. Stanton, observing that 'This is a ridiculous case,' said he would consider his next move. Actually, he had already made it: well within his own garden, planted a few yards behind the controversial hedge (now 22 feet high and 8 feet thick) is a sturdy new row of tiny ×*Cupressocyparis leylandii.*

Ivy

The English are great ones for starting debates, usually in the correspondence columns of certain magazines and newspapers. In fact, they are perfectly capable of inventing arguments out of sheet cussedness. Where an American might dash off an angry letter about some straightforward issue like secondhand smoke or a malfunctioning traffic light, Disgusted of Tunbridge Wells is likely to huff and puff about an excess of magpies or demand to know what the government intends to do about crop circles. When enough letters have appeared, pro and con, the argument generally graduates into a news story as soufflé-like as the original dispute.

A few weeks ago, in just this way, the Ivy Argument emerged again. It started with a letter to *Country Life* from one Philip Robinson of Stone Hall, Great Mongeham, Deal, Kent. 'What shall be done,' Mr Robinson asked, 'to preserve our all too small number of deciduous trees' from being smothered and killed by ivy? 'The countryside is full of disfigured and dying woodland,' all because of the failure of landowners and local authorities to clean up their trees. It was (naturally) a matter of 'urgent concern'.

Now, while *Hedera helix*, the common English ivy (and, incidentally, Britain's only native evergreen climber), is not quite in a class with the kudzu vine, there's no doubt about its rampancy. 'Ivy-covered cottage' may be a poetic concept, but it is also a frightening reality to those concerned about their gutters and roof slates. In the woods, ivy seems to wriggle up the trunks of most trees while your back is turned, converting what was once a nice little ash, say, into a great mop-headed ivy-leafed lollipop. When a strong wind comes along, the whole overloaded mass of greenery – ivy, tree, birds' nests and all – may very well keel over.

Mr Robinson's *cri de coeur* certainly struck a sympathetic note with me. Only a few months earlier, we had spent a couple of winter afternoons chopping wrist-thick ropes of ivy running up the trunks of larches in our wood. We gave up after dealing with the most obvious candidates for stripping. Ivy has to be prised free of the trunk before you can cut it, and in any case you can't pull down more than 10 feet or so. The rest, separated from its roots, simply dies up there (and, one hopes, eventually sheds its dead, dried leaves). The basic point of the exercise was to make the wood look more like a wood and less like a solid mass of shiny green leaves, but I suppose that in the backs of our minds we were also going along with the notion that ivy is inherently destructive – to walls, buildings, roots and, above all, to trees, by strangling, smothering, weakening or even poisoning. Ivy as murderer, in other words.

In this we were following the lead of possibly the most distinguished of all ivy antagonists – Queen Mary, then the Queen Mother. In 1939, moving to Gloucestershire on the outbreak of war, she promptly organized an 'Ivy Squad' devoted to stripping trees and walls. Nobody could evade the duty – equerries, courtiers, visitors, various gardeners and servants were all enrolled. When they ran out of ivy they turned to clearing brush and thinning trees. (The Queen insisted on riding to work in a farm cart. One day someone remarked that she looked as if she were in a tumbrel. 'Well, it may come to that,' she replied. 'One never knows.')

Queen Mary's position on ivy – her conviction that the plant would pull down brickwork and sap the strength of trees – is one that Mr Robinson clearly shares. But no argument is one-sided, and Robinson's letter was soon followed in *Country Life* by defences of ivy, whose authors included Andrew Craves of the Kent Trust for Nature Conservation. In a voice ringing with authority, he declared that ivy does not kill trees; it is a climbing vine, not a parasite. Its suckers do not penetrate the bark. Furthermore, it pulls down trees only if they are already dying. Bats, birds and invertebrates find shelter among its stems and leaves, and its flowers provide nectar. All in all, as another correspondent wrote, 'one should be thankful for its presence'.

One might as well be. There is far too much ivy in this country, and it grows far too vigorously, for any official position to develop, pro or con. The Forestry Commission publishes booklets on grey-squirrel control, starling-roost dispersal and 'Weeding in the Forest', but not a word on ivy. *The Forester's Companion*'s only mention of ivy is its listing – along with honeysuckle, *Clematis vitalba*, gorse and bracken – as a harmful plant that ought to be cut down on sight. On the other hand, John White, the Forestry Commission's chief dendrologist, is quoted in *The Times* as saying that 'ivy is not a killer. It is not parasitic and there is no direct damage to the tree. As ground cover, in fact, it protects the woodland floor from hard frost and enables ground-foraging birds and mammals to continue feeding during the winter.'

If there is a middle ground here, it probably lies in a better understanding than most people have (certainly better than I had until I began reading up on the subject) about ivy itself and the way it grows. In her definitive and very beautiful book *Ivies*, Jane Fearnley-Whittingstall points out that ivy actually has the capacity (read 'fearful tendency', if you choose) to be two entirely different kinds of plant.

To start with, it is a self-clinging climber that crawls along the ground, rooting as it goes, until it finds something vertical to ascend. Then, in familiar ivy fashion, it grows upward along the trunk of a tree or across the face of a wall, sending out hairy rootlets that adhere tightly to any slightly rough surface. When it can climb no higher, it stops, sending out long, graceful tendrils, without rootlets, and generally behaving in a civilized way.

At this point, however, it undergoes a sort of Jekyll–Hyde transformation into what is technically termed an 'arborescent' form. In other words, it becomes tree-like. The juvenile ivy graduates into adulthood. It produces a new sort of leaf, smooth-edged and rounded where the earlier leaves were lobed and sharp-pointed, and these gradually appear over the entire plant. A new growth pattern emerges – shrubby, stoutly branched, dense and distinctly *heavy*. For the birds there are plenty of berries now and, for the connoisseur of aerial flowers, a yearly autumnal display of greenish-yellow blossoms. But for the poor tree trying to support all this in its crown, life is difficult, if not actually over.

Thus it is in its arborescence that ivy poses the most serious threat to trees. Obviously a tree that is already weak is at greatest risk of falling; a sick tree with thinning foliage will most likely make it easy for a rampantly healthy ivy to fulfil its natural destiny. (An ash, which leafs out relatively late in the spring, and even then does not cast a deep shade, is notably more likely to harbour ivy than a beech is.) Mrs Fearnley-Whittingstall suggests that it is only common sense to trim back ivy on a vulnerable tree to prevent it reaching the crown and turning arborescent.

But she confirms that a lot of the other complaints about ivy are not fair. The rootlets that cause it to cling to walls and bark are not true roots searching for moisture or nutrients, so they won't loosen sound mortar or invade the tree. (Defective mortar or cracked bricks are another matter. Ivy rootlets can pull them apart.) Ivy leaves cloaking a house may help insulate it and, by throwing off rain and snow, prevent weathering. The leaves are *not* poisonous, in spite of rumours to that effect – probably the result of confusion with poison ivy (which isn't an ivy, and doesn't grow over here anyway).

As a clincher, Mrs Fearnley-Whittingstall quotes the findings of an experiment in which half the oaks in a woodland plot were cleaned of ivy every ten years, starting in 1890, and the others left to suffer. In 1942, when the plot was logged off, no difference in height, girth or average cubic content could be discerned between the two samples.

My own position in the Ivy Argument is one of sympathetic neutrality. It's a phony debate in any case. Clearly, the stuff is not going to wipe out the British woods. Yet there is no way around its basically scruffy and independent nature. Picturesque it may be, but an ivy-clad tree is bound to look neglected. At the same time, ivy has many attractions as a garden plant. Cuttings (known as 'tree-ivies') taken from an arborescent specimen can be grown as shrubs; they won't revert to their juvenile climbing form (though it is difficult to get them to strike in the first place, I'm told). And the climbing versions come in a huge variety of shapes, colours and habits. As with so many other gardening questions, the real issue seems to be personal taste.

It should be said, as Eleanor Perenyi (a great ivy fancier) has, that unless the climate is mild (like ours over here), ivy is very unlikely to reach arborescence. In New England, the juvenile vines usually suffer from winterkill, and years of uninterrupted growth (she says thirty, though this sounds excessive) are needed before the sea-change occurs. This no doubt explains the comparative rarity of smothered trees in the Berkshires.

When we first came to Towerhill Cottage, the remains of a hedge bordering the lawn consisted in large part of a clump of ivy (arborescent, I now realize) about the size of a small moving van. At its heart was the crumpled trunk of a tree. For several years I looked at this thing, trying to find something to admire – its glossy leaves? Its blue-black berries? The way it so efficiently prevented the everlasting south-west wind from slicing through the shrub bed? In the end I failed. An hour's work with lopping shears and axe did the job, and we've never missed it.

The same goes for the ivy stripped off those larches. They look happier without it, and they're certainly more elegant. But just in case things seem to be getting a little too bare, I've been contemplating the west wall of the house. It occurs to me that a nice bit of *Hedera helix* 'Green Ripple' would look smashing there.

Ancient Woods

Just across our lane we have an authentic Ancient Wood. It is called Dreinos Wood ('dreinos' means 'thorny' or 'brambly' in Welsh), and to my knowledge it has been there, called by that name, since at least the beginning of the seventeenth century. It appears on a map said to be Elizabethan, which is framed on the wall of the Skenfrith village church. It is also mentioned a couple of times in a survey made around 1610 for the Duchy of Lancaster, at which time it was leased by Charles Morgan, gent., and covered about 8 acres.

These days Dreinos Wood has shrunk to no more than 2 or 3 acres. In recent years grazing land for sheep has been worth more than trees. But the wood still contains a few big oaks, and the ashes that make up the bulk of it are huge and handsome specimens, towering high above the lane and affording perfect nesting sites for a colony of rooks. Rookeries tend to stay put; I wouldn't be surprised to learn that the ancestors of these same lugubrious birds were swooping and cawing here when Henry V was born down the road in Monmouth. There is something deeply affecting about a rookery, always more active in a late-autumn or spring gale, with the bare treetops thrashing and the great ragged nests 'swinging like wrecks in a stormy sea', as Dickens put it in *David Copperfield*.

Technically, an Ancient Wood is a wood that was already in existence by 1700. The date is not quite arbitrary. Oliver Rackham, the great historian of the English countryside, points out that medieval tree-management systems survived in Britain until relatively recently, so any piece of woodland that was around in 1700 had probably been around in more or less the same form for a long time before that. In fact, according to Rackham, such a wood is almost certainly a remnant of the original primary forest that existed in prehistoric times, long before the Angles and the Saxons and even the Romans.

That a wood is ancient doesn't necessarily mean it is full of big old trees. On the contrary. The oldest trees in Dreinos Wood don't appear to be more than a century or a century and a half old. Far older – and bigger – trees, tremendous oaks absolutely knotted with age, can be found scattered in hedgerows and meadows all around us. What particularly distinguishes an Ancient Wood is the fact that during the greater part of its very long life, it has been *managed*.

In most of England, and in the Welsh Marches where we live, woodland was traditionally regarded as an important renewable resource. Besides providing food for pigs (the size of a beech or oak wood might be described in terms of 'pannage' – how many pigs it would support), a practice called coppicing maximized the amount of wood that could be produced. This meant allowing a tree to send up a cluster of relatively small trunks, which were then harvested on a regular basis, say every fifteen or twenty years, to supply everything from building materials to scythe handles to firewood – even ash for making soap or pottery glazes. Another technique, pollarding, involves cutting off all the branches to leave a stubbly lump perched atop the trunk: a familiar, if ugly, sight to anyone who has travelled in France, and an expedient still occasionally adopted here to keep rampant plane trees in check. Simply chopping down a full-grown tree and sawing it up for boards and firewood was regarded as wasteful or worse – depending on who you were, it could land you in the stocks or on a gallows.

A regularly coppiced tree can, moreover, survive almost indefinitely. Left to itself, Rackham observes, an ash tree will live 200 years and then fall down, allowing some other species to take its place. But, if coppiced, it might well go on growing in the same spot after 500 or 1,000 years. Even now you don't have to hunt very far through a piece of ancient woodland to find evidence of coppicing in times past – no single stump, but a vaguely circular eruption of small trunks and rotting stumps sometimes 10 or 20 feet in diameter.

Nobody, so far as I know, is doing any coppicing in our neighbourhood these days, the market for ash and hazel wands to weave into sheep hurdles having fallen off. Firewood has been largely replaced by bottled gas, except for fireplace sentimentalists like us (and we use gas to cook with). So while I'm delighted by the survival of Dreinos Wood, its rooks and its springtime bluebells, its fate is clearly somewhat problematic. Major Mitchley, the owner of the wood, is no longer able to chop brambles with a billhook, and those big ashes won't withstand the south-west winds indefinitely.

Rackham maintains that there may be no such thing as a really *natural* ancient wood. Without the kind of tinkering represented by coppicing, certain lovely and familiar species would probably have been replaced long since. Ash, in our neighbourhood, seems to spring up pretty much without encouragement everywhere (including the middle of flower borders), but hornbeam will knock out hazel if coppicing stops, and such weed trees as aspen and wild cherry can overpower young beech. So when you come right down to it, the sort of traditional English wood we associate with Winnie-the-Pooh and *The Wind in the Willows* is as artificial – and precious – as Westminster Abbey. Rather more typical, I'm afraid, is my own wood, much of which is already falling down. It consists of about 2 acres, mainly planted to larch, a very gloomy conifer, which – on top of everything else – manages to lose its needles in the winter. Before coming here I was unacquainted with larches, and I do not prize their discovery. These particular trees were planted in a flush of hopefulness by a previous owner exactly forty-eight years ago, no doubt inspired by a post-war shortage of timber. I am now in a position to testify that the normal lifespan of a larch is about forty-eight years, and that a full-grown larch isn't worth much, especially when it is hung up in another tree and can't be chainsawed without imperilling the sawyer. It even makes dubious firewood, since, like most conifers, it has a habit of exploding on the hearth.

One solution would be to clear-cut and start all over again. This is the strategy favoured by my neighbour Jimmy McConnel, who, in addition to farming several hundred acres of blackcurrants and cider-apple trees, now owns a considerable tract of hillside closely planted by the Forestry Commission, years ago, with fir and spruce. McConnel's trees are ready to be logged off. I suggested to him that he might like to leave the few old sweet chestnuts and oaks scattered through the conifers, but as a practical man who earns his living harvesting things, he quite rightly declined. Clear-cutting is a lot more efficient. Judging from a section he logged a few years ago, the place will look like the Western Front in 1916 for a while, but it's amazing to see the wildflowers that emerge once the sun reaches the ground. Exceptional blackberries, too. And just as soon as the tractors are finished, he'll replant.

I would rather not clear-cut, however. Mixed with the larches in my wood I've discovered an assortment of broadleaf trees – oak, ash, beech, some birch and hazel. Some of them are already well grown, especially along the edges of the wood, which is long and very narrow. The only way I could hope to save them would be to cut the larches one at a time, snaking the logs carefully out into the meadows alongside. If I could find a man with a draught horse or two, it would be a cinch. Then I'd get in there with a brush cutter, clear out the brambles, bracken and wild roses, and give the bluebells a chance. Instant Ancient Wood.

A newspaper story some months ago suggests that my fantasy is shared by people thinking on a far larger scale. Tim Yeo, then the Countryside Minister (yes, we have one of those), announced plans to plant 30 million trees, two-thirds of them broadleaf, in a new national forest covering 200 square miles of Derbyshire, Leicestershire and Staffordshire. It will take thirty years and cost up to £4 million a year (although, ominously, the article points out that 'no detailed decisions on funding have yet been taken'). Before it begins to look like a proper wood, of course, we'll have to wait at least half a century. This is too long for me and, probably, Tim Yeo (who, I note, has since lost his job).

To anyone who has lived in New England, such an enterprise is bound to seem a bit laborious. Woods just *grow*, don't they? Abandoned land, as Rackham points out, inevitably 'tumbles down to woodland'. Yet a patch of scrub elder can hardly be compared with the majesty of an old managed wood. Moreover there seems to be something deeply instinctive and conservative about the British feeling for trees. It isn't simply that business about a new national forest – almost every day brings some new story about protestors barricaded in tree houses or chaining themselves to a threatened oak, or about the launch of yet another survey to locate and catalogue all examples of a rare species, the wild service tree (*Sorbus terminalis*) or the black poplar (*Populus nigra betufolia*). It's as if the landscape is simply too small and valuable to permit carelessness, or a loss of control, even on the part of nature. Or man, for that matter — there has been a huge backlash against the practice of block-planting vast expanses of wild moorland with conifers.

Such arborial devotion may strike many Americans as excessive (after all, we had to chop our way through an awful lot of trees before achieving what we regard as civilization), but this American has been converted. You simply can't argue with the beauty of thin light falling through the leaves of an Ancient Wood, or the stately authority of an aged oak tree in a meadow. In my opinion they are worth a bit of crankiness, and it's catching.

Flowers of the Forest

It is now early May, the best time of all in this part of the world, and the bluebells are marching through open tracts of the woods, a dazzling carpet of cerulean colour that seems to echo the sky above. You just can't be nonchalant about wildflowers like these. There is nothing at all retiring or modest about them, no 'flower-in-the-crannied-wall' quality, yet at the same time there is nothing exotic either. They look as though they were invented in the first place to enhance the glory of young beech leaves, or to refract and enliven the mild light that filters into an English woodland in spring. They belong here, natives of the dappled shade.

Anyone entering a bluebell wood for the first time is bound to be struck by the way the plants form dense pools of colour, massed panicles of drooping bells that can blanket whole stretches of the forest floor. The droop itself is distinctive. The poet Gerard Manley Hopkins remarked upon it in his journal in May 1873: 'Bluebells in Hodder Wood, all hanging their heads one way. I noted as well as I could . . . the level or stage or shire of colour they make hanging in the air a foot above the grass . . .' Yet it is the intensity of the colour in shade that really strikes us, Hopkins's 'falls of sky-colour'. While white blue-bells are common enough, a solid warm blue in the depths of a wood is what comes first to mind when bluebells are mentioned. I was a little surprised to learn the other day that bluebells don't need to grow in a wood. Walking over a hill near Tower-hill Cottage, we came upon a rough sheep meadow sloping steeply out of an oak-and-ash forest. It was covered with thousands of bluebells. They were far more scattered, and comparatively austere – only a bell or two per plant, against six to ten for their burly luscious woodland counterparts – and the effect was less a thunderous blue than an extraordinary blue-green glaze across the field. At first, from a distance, I thought they were an expanse of dog violets.

According to Richard Mabey, whose expertise on and love for the British countryside has borne fruit in several fascinating books, bluebells growing outside a wood in open country like this are actually a sign that the area was once covered with trees. Provided the place is damp and mild enough, bluebells will linger on, sometimes for many years, after the trees have been cleared away. I have no doubt that this explains their presence on the side of Coedangred Hill, and probably also their slightly stressed growth pattern as year by year the ground there fills in with grass and bracken and dries out.

So, as Mabey points out, bluebells enjoy shade but do not actually *need* it. In fact, what they like best is a periodic refreshing dose of sunlight, whereupon they spread and flower most luxuriantly. The ideal is a regularly coppiced wood cleared of most young growth every twenty years or so. This has been going on in some English woods for a thousand years or longer. As noted in the preceding chapter, however, nobody is doing much coppicing these days and hasn't been since the 1920s.

You have to wonder what this means to all the other classic British woodland wildflowers, like primroses, oxlips and anemones. Oliver Rackham points out that large communities of such plants have survived mainly because of their access to an alternating cycle of sun and shade. They don't like permanent heavy shade, but full sun endangers them too by allowing more vigorous and aggressive species – brackens, grasses, and brambles – to smother them. Even worse is the prospect of existence within conifer plantations, the sort of dismal, regimented tree farms that have defaced so much of the landscape since World War II. It is a bit hard to imagine an anemone, or any other bit of flora short of a toadstool, enjoying life in the dark, acid, needle-choked earth beneath an army of firs. (Mabey reports a study showing that the seeds of herbaceous flowers and shrubs can survive for up to fourteen years under accumulating layers of toxic pine litter, but after that it's curtains.)

Many people have commented on the decline in the numbers of wild primroses (*Primula vulgaris*). No doubt this is true, although as a relative newcomer to the scene I'm not in a position to judge. You still see the odd one along the verge of shady lanes, among the celandine. But I have never spotted a primrose growing in the woods, where they are supposed to. (There are plenty of escaped polyanthuses around, of course, but for these purposes they don't count.) The Victorian curate Francis Kilvert, who lived not far from us a century ago, has a delightful passage in his diary about the local custom of gathering armloads of wildflowers from 'the primrose- and anemone-starred woods' to decorate the village church and the graves in the churchyard for Easter Sunday. 'Here and there,' he writes, 'the banks and road sides were spangled with primroses and they shone like stars among the little brakes and bramble thickets overhanging the brook.' Today, I suspect, he might have a tougher, if not necessarily hopeless, time of it. Yet even here renewed coppicing could do much to improve matters. When a Cambridgeshire wood was experimentally restored to coppicing in 1955, the primrose population responded with a positively hysterical burst of flowering that lasted eighteen months and produced a 1,000 per cent increase in blooms.

It's likely to take more than the end of coppicing to kill off Britain's bluebells. They can be persistent little things. The first ones I ever ran across grew in our London back garden, and there it was never a question of *cultivating* them; on the contrary, we spent most of our bluebell time trying to get rid of them. They seed readily, and their small, deep bulbs are the very devil to locate and expunge. Let them go and soon – logically – you've got something resembling a bluebell wood where your garden used to be.

Similarly, there is abundant evidence of the ability of many plants to adapt to, or even take advantage of, the conditions created deliberately or ignorantly by man. When we first came to Towerhill Cottage, our view – now 10 clear miles or so to the Trellech Ridge – was completely obscured by a scruffy quarter-acre growth of elder, grey birch, blackberry and wild-rose canes and what remained of a hedge that had been growing unclipped for ten or fifteen years. This stuff I cut down, burned and – eventually – started mowing. The first year, before the grass got going, we had a fairly uninspiring spread of bare earth studded with incipient brambles that didn't know they had been beaten. The second year, though, was miraculous – a low-lying blue fog of forget-me-nots emerged wherever the grass was still stunted. Since then the grass has begun getting the upper hand, but the forget-me-nots – with no help at all from us – have blown into all the flower beds and happily billow there each spring before their cultivated companions deign to blossom.

Among wildflowers probably nothing could be more authentically English than cowslips, which accounts for the dismay that arose a few years ago over reports that they were dying out.

Today, however, these splendid plants, which throw up great clusters of rich yellow cups at the top of strong vertical stalks, are turning up in the most unlikely and improbable places. There is a nice patch in a cutting on the Monmouth road a couple of miles south of us. W. D. Campbell, writing in the *Guardian* recently, theorized that since cowslip seeds are unlikely to be spread by either wind or birds, they probably survive a long period of dormancy before cultivation or climate leads to their germination. The sight of a native woodland cowslip springing up in a crack in a cement path must be telling us something.

One of my favourite examples of the way plants take advantage of man's disruption of habitat is the nettle-phosphate nexus. Nettles – the big, tall, stinging kind – crave phosphates. Human beings, Rackham points out, are 'phosphate-accumulating animals'. In other words, we collect phosphate from the food we eat and concentrate it in our bones and our excreta. Where people have lived (and especially died) over many generations, you therefore find nettles growing in abundance. You can even use them as indications of long-vanished settlements, rather like lilacs in the middle of New England woods. Little Gidding, a ghost village in Huntingdonshire that was deserted and forgotten by 1640, still has an elm grove full of 5-foot-tall nettles. And if there were ever any doubt about how long people have been living on our own small piece of land, I (regrettably) have the nettles to prove that it has been a very long time indeed.

There are a few other plants that, like nettles, choose their homes on the basis of phosphate deposits left by humans – elderberry bushes and goosegrass (cleavers), for example. Personally, I'm not thrilled by the prospect of encouraging the spread of any more of these. I'd rather have some harebells, a fritillary or two and perhaps a selection of orchids. Yet these are exactly the kinds of plant most threatened – possibly terminally – by human activity. Each of these beauties seems to need something that is in shorter and shorter supply – precisely the right amount of moisture, shade but not too much, a long-settled habitat or simply peace and quiet.

In one corner of our orchard, partly sheltered by an old apple tree and some hedgerow alders whose shade inhibits grass, we have discovered a small colony of early purple orchids (*Orchis maculata*). This variety is not very rare; in fact, it may be the most common orchid of all, scorned by those connoisseurs who relish a military orchid or a bird's nest orchid. But we regard it as a prize. You can't do much for any kind of orchid except leave it alone, which we are doing assiduously. I'm glad to say that each year a few more little purple spikes appear. I'd love to have a bluebell wood, but I'll settle for an orchid orchard.

Garden Visiting

Contrary to sentimental assumptions, the favourite summertime sport in the English countryside isn't cricket. It's garden visiting. By that I don't mean the world-renowned big spreads, like Hidcote, or Chatsworth, or Sissinghurst – there are dozens of these, of course, and heaven knows people (especially foreign tourists) pour through them in chattering floods, rain or shine, all summer long. The visits that we and millions of locals really enjoy are to the less famous and usually more modest private gardens listed and described in what everybody calls 'the Yellow Book', the handbook of the National Gardens Scheme.

The National Gardens Scheme itself, that godsend to the horticulturally nosy, dates back to 1927, when a Miss Elsie Wagg suggested that inviting people to show off their otherwise private gardens on a day or two a year – they could choose the day – would be a fine way to raise money for good causes. The first year 600 gardens opened, and £8,191 was raised. Today the Scheme involves some 3,500 gardens (660 more this year alone), and the take is in the order of £1.6 million, divided up between charities like the Queen's Nursing Institute and the Royal Gardeners' Orphan Fund. Some also goes, appropriately, to the National Trust for helping to maintain gardens of special interest (also listed in the Yellow Book). The Book tells you how to get there, provides a short description ('wellingtons advisable') and lists opening times.

All this sounds terribly large-scale and formal, but the beauty of the Gardens Scheme really lies in its intimacy. A lot of the people you see at a 'Garden Open' day are neighbours, happy to pay a couple of pounds for a good snoop. Ladies from the local Women's Institute or church group generally run a plant stand, with (if you're lucky) some oddities among the pelargoniums, and serve the TEA or TEAS. (The Yellow Book explains this subtle but important distinction. TEA gets you a cupful and a couple of Peek Frean biscuits; TEAS, more substantial, promise homemade cakes and maybe even a cucumber sandwich. To an Englishman such things can make all the difference. Judging from the numbers seen guzzling in sheltered corners, I have a sneaking suspicion that many visitors come for the TEAS alone.) Some of the profits from these enterprises may be siphoned off to mend the church roof or restore the 1914–1918 war memorial.

Despite some nervousness about potential burglars scouting the property, plenty of gardeners are eager to get their gardens listed in the Yellow Book. Each county in England and Wales (Scotland's Gardens Scheme is separate) has its own 'organizer' (a big, garden-rich county like Dorset may have half a dozen assistant organizers too, and perhaps a treasurer), whose responsibility it is to choose the gardens to be included and make sure that they stay up to snuff. This can be a challenging task, since the rules are very loose. The only rule, in fact, seems to be that, to be included, a garden should be of sufficient interest to occupy a visitor for forty minutes. An organizer can use his or her own judgement about what is interesting. Or isn't: 'If all it has is rows and rows of salvias, people aren't going to think it's worth the trip,' observes Mariel Toynbee, county organizer for

Buckinghamshire. One of an organizer's more painful tasks is breaking the news to a proud garden owner that his roses must blush unseen after all.

But the latitude granted to the organizers has the pleasant effect of offering the garden visitor an amazing variety of places to invade. Some are tiny and choked with extraordinary collections of unusual plants. Others may be large and fairly grand, with sweeping views across old parkland (classics like Powis Castle and Petworth have their Gardens Scheme days too). There are town gardens where everything is in pots, and rural gardens specializing in vegetables (organic, natch). You can visit rose breeder David Austin's own rose garden (move smartly – it's open for only four hours on a single afternoon), or, if you'd rather, Rupert Brooke's garden at the Old Vicarage in Grantchester, now owned by that other literary giant, Jeffrey Archer. A single £2.50 ticket will get you into seven different gardens in Ely in Cambridgeshire on a day in June.

Of course, the strain on the owners of very small gardens can be intense. 'Please visit throughout the day to ease pressure' is a common refrain in Yellow Book entries, and many gardens are open only by appointment because they lack parking space. (In this respect Walpole House on Chiswick Mall in London has an exceptional problem: the owners must select their opening days on the basis of tide tables, so that garden visitors' parked cars are not inadvertently submerged by high tides running up the Thames.) But the satisfaction of knowing that your garden qualifies for inclusion tends to overcome a lot of sensible inhibitions. And for visitors there is always the joy of the chase. You never know quite what you'll run into.

For example, one Sunday last summer we drove over into Gloucestershire to visit two gardens. The first, called Camp Cottage, was promisingly described in the Yellow Book as 'a plant-lover's seventeenth-century cottage garden' covering about three-quarters of an acre, with 'old roses, pergola with arches, climbing plants, many unusual plants . . .' All of this turned out to be true – the Yellow Book entries, though generally written by the garden owners themselves, are invariably accurate, if sometimes inadequate – but hardly prepared us for what we found.

The house, a thatched dwelling (I choose the word deliberately for its hobbitesque associations), was literally overwhelmed by its garden. Clematis, vines of various sorts, *Hydrangea petiolaris*, wisteria, honeysuckle – you name it, it was clambering over the cottage, which you could hardly see. Tiny irregular plots of grass (irregularly mowed and edged, too) vainly attempted to separate beds overflowing with herbaceous plants in no particular order, but obviously very happy and flowering abundantly. Small fruit trees drooped over settlements of rare shade lovers. Stone troughs harboured alpines. And the roses! From rough arbours built of bark on poles cascaded a brilliant variety of climbing roses in such profusion that you almost had to make your way through the garden on all fours. Embracing the whole place was a dense stand of trees and bushes (probably hedges surrendered to the elements many years ago) that succeeded in cutting out most of the noise from the nearby highway, and ought to have cut out most of the sun to the roses too, but apparently didn't. I don't believe I've ever seen a smaller three-quarters of an acre.

On the same afternoon, we went to Ryelands House, a handsome Queen Anne mansion only a few miles away, where a courtly retired gentleman named Captain Eldred Wilson and his deeply knowledgeable wife have created a garden of a radically different kind. Its key element is a sunken expanse of lawn entered by flights of old formal steps overhung by ancient trees and bordered by clipped yew hedges. A brook filled with water plants runs through the lower portion; there are bowers of climbing roses; herbaceous borders; and, in the spring, beds of crocuses, tulips and daffodils. Daffodils, in fact, are a speciality of Ryelands; in the hillside meadows behind the house, along the edges of the wood where visitors are invited to walk, colonies of wild daffodils survive.

Ryelands is not large – including the lawns, I suppose the garden proper extends to no more than a couple of acres. Yet the sense of spaciousness is strong, encouraged by the open country all around. The Wilsons have consciously kept everything in scale, permitting concentration upon detail, maintaining the grounds in first-rate order and experimenting with particularly rare varieties of plants, some of which are for sale. What we carried home with us that day, along with the predictable feelings of envy, was a single white crane's-bill geranium that has turned out, this summer, to be downright exquisite.

Exposed to such an abundance of horticulture, amateur and professional, it is difficult to avoid getting fussy. During the six or eight years we've been using the Yellow Book to explore gardens in our area we've seen all sorts. We have visited show-off gardens where every blade of grass is in its ordained place (never a buttercup, much less a nettle); *nouveaux riches* gardens ordered, ready-made, from a designer and rolled out like carpeting; beloved gardens showing years – generations sometimes – of hand labour; inherited gardens sustained by dwindling trust funds; gardens that haven't quite come off yet but are trying oh-so-hard. We have seen gardens worth imitating and gardens we couldn't leave fast enough. We have also come upon gardens that give you a sudden view into what gardening is all about, the eternally fascinating interplay between human enterprise and wild nature.

Early in April, on a blustery but sunny day, we noticed in the Yellow Book that Garnons was open. Garnons is a big house just east of Hereford, perched on a hillside, that you can see at a distance from the road. The Book's description (presumably written by Sir John Cotterell himself) was typically laconic: 'Attractive spring garden . . . large park landscaped by Repton'. The house didn't sound like much – 'Remaining wing (1860) of house pulled down in 1957'. But it was a nice day, and the earth in *our* garden was still too cold and wet to be worked. So we went to Garnons.

It was a revelation. The drive up to the house winds through Humphry Repton's park, now 200 years old, studded with tremendous oaks and beeches and mowed by grazing sheep. The house itself is nothing like the 'wing' of something else but a handsome stone block with large, beautiful windows, a castellated roofline, and wisteria, ceanothus, chaenomeles and pyracantha cloaking the walls. From the terraces in front the views extended at least 10 miles, down into the valley of the Wye and up again to the Black Mountains far beyond, while formal rose beds, barely beginning to leaf out, patterned the flagged levels on the east side of the house.

The 'spring garden' actually consisted of an entire hillside to the west of the house, a great tangle of trees and shrubs and bulbs in bloom. There were vast drifts of daffodils and polyanthuses in the grass (which had not yet begun its early-summer burst of growth), half a dozen different kinds of flowering cherries, leviathan oaks and beeches, a huge elm, banks of rhododendrons (a white one already breaking into precocious bloom), philadelphuses, dogwoods, daphnes. Pathways ran more or less at random, up the hill and across it; there were some signs, but not many, of discreet pruning and ground clearing. Clearly, the whole thing didn't have much order in it. Yet somehow it was the very essence of a spring landscape – natural, fresh, alight with promise – a garden likely to stick in the mind longer, perhaps, than a more controlled and conventional one.

At the moment, it's hard to imagine that we'll ever manage to see everything the Yellow Book has on offer in our vicinity. And if by any chance we do, we can always start all over. That's one of the lovely things about gardens – they never stay the same. Nor does the visitor.

*

Most garden visitors are gardeners. There's no point in being too snooty about it – we traipse around in a haze of admiration and envy and (most likely) the conviction that there, but for the ungraciousness of God, go we. After all, next to actually gardening, the average gardener is happiest showing off his or her garden to other people. You don't have to spend many Sunday afternoons on tour before you start wondering whether maybe your own garden might measure up.

This being Britain, a sort of unofficial pecking order has developed to govern garden visiting. Some gardens are obviously more equal than others. At the bottom of the list will be gardens suitable only for visits by family friends and relatives and potentially destructive dogs. A step higher are gardens qualifying for an 'open village' day of the sort that Garway had a few weeks ago – you buy a ticket (proceeds to the church fund) and then tour all the gardens in the village. Some of these can be very fine. But the real *gratin* of gardens are those that turn up in the Yellow Book. To those of us who care, getting your garden accepted for this is an authentic Big Deal, an OBE, say, if not quite a knighthood.

While I admit that the garden of Towerhill Cottage may not be quite ready for inclusion yet, I can't resist exploring how far we have to go. (I'm sure you know the feeling – it's a bit like doing those little puzzles that tell you whether you qualify for Mensa.) Fortunately, we have an objective standard to go by, that forty-minute-interest minimum decreed by the National Gardens Scheme. Let's see how it adds up.

I begin my assessment with the **meadow**. This consists of 1 acre of moderately rough grass, a pear tree (Conference) and, at the moment, two sheep. It is not flat but slightly bulging, which adds piquancy to the view. Say, *one* minute, *two* if you like sheep. (Parenthetically, I should note that I used to like sheep more than I do now, ever since a Suffolk Cross ram and I had a difference of opinion about who was more deserving of the pears. I got the pears, but at a cost of four sessions with a physiotherapist to restore my back to working condition after the ram butted me.)

The **lawns**. There are several lawns (probably too many). The smoothest and least buttercup-beset has a serious mole problem. We call it the croquet lawn because somebody once tried to play croquet on it, although miniature golf might have worked better. From a distance, however, and freshly mowed, this is a pretty lawn. A connoisseur might spend *three* minutes gazing at it. The other lawns feature dandelions, more buttercups, speedwells, daisies and, in season, a fine crop of greater celandines. And, of course, molehills. Generously, *two* minutes for the lot.

Trees. We have some lovely trees. I can claim credit for them only in the most technical sense, since they have been living here a lot longer than we have. Among them is a magnificent English walnut (tons of nuts, virtually all scoffed by squirrels at the instant of ripeness); a huge lime resembling a Brobdingnagian bush because nobody ever tried to reduce it to a single trunk, and now it's too late; and a selection of beeches and oaks of varying size and visibility. There is also a long, narrow wood

amounting to a couple of acres, composed largely of superannu-
ated larches. They show this by falling down. A crash in the
wood means another two months of logs for the fire. This may
not be approved forestry practice, but it's safer than felling them
myself. If you have a taste for brambles and underbrush, the
wood might interest you for about *five* minutes. I'd say *two*, plus
another *two* for the rest of the trees.

The **shrubs**. Consider the rhododendrons first. If this were
New England, our rhododendrons would be a prize. We have a
big bank of them, blazingly magenta in May. Around here,
though, rhododendrons like these are, as they say, two a penny.
More of a menace than an ornament. Once they get started, it
takes a billhook to stop them. I know this because I spent most
of a day last year reducing the size of the bank by half. In hopes
of introducing a note of civility here, we have planted some
proper rhododendrons, deep scarlet and white. The white are
fine, the scarlet died suddenly. *Zero* (half a minute for the good
rhododendrons, minus half a minute for the magenta monsters).

The rest of the shrubs (mostly planted in the bed retrieved by
the billhook) are fairly miscellaneous – hydrangeas, a ceanothus
taking the form of a tree, potentillas, several blueberry bushes,
lavateras. All of them except the blueberries (which would
apparently rather be in Massachusetts) seem altogether happy.
In fact, if we don't do some forceful transplanting soon, a
wrestling match may break out between a buddleia and a couple
of exceptionally muscular fuchsias. In six or eight years this
bed will be sheltered from the south-west wind by a beech
hedge, if the south-west wind doesn't get the beech hedge first.
For this admirable shrub bed, *five* minutes.

The **herbaceous border**. This is Carol's territory. She has
restored it from an existing raised bed filled with a tangled mass
of vegetation, including a fatsia growing on top of a knotted old

species rose, some peonies that had lost their way, bits of candy-tuft, a fine stand of Japanese anemones and quite a few stones. I would like to report that this bed has been completely reorganized and replanted. It hasn't, because it still awaits integration into a larger scheme (see below). But it is now basically weed-free, thanks to the billows of foliage and blossoms, which are as cottage-gardeny as anyone could wish. *Five* minutes.

The **view**. I'm very proud of our view because I opened it up myself by hacking down the half-acre of nettles and man-high blackberry brambles that was obstructing it. It now extends from the house down a slope, across a hedge and fields of blackcurrant and oilseed rape, to wooded hills 20 miles away, taking in an assortment of mountains, farmhouses and electric pylons. Personally, I think the view is worth a half-hour of anybody's time, except when it's raining and you can't see beyond the hedge, but to be fair I'd better make it *four* minutes. It isn't, strictly speaking, a garden feature but more a gift from heaven.

The **allée**. The objective critic would probably say that the allée has not yet achieved its full potential. It is a strip of one-time green lane about 10 feet wide and 60 feet long that I have been mowing to discourage the nettles. We have planted the odd shrub along the sides – mahonias, japonicas, lilacs, a couple of camellias – most of which have died or been mowed by mistake. One thing that might help is a piece of statuary – say, a nice marble Diana or perhaps an effigy of Gertrude Jekyll. Instead there are at the moment two steel stakes in the middle, nicely placed to trip the unobservant. These comprise the only horseshoe-pitching court in Wales, possibly the entirety of Britain. At one end of the allée are two heaps of sheep manure, a cheering sight to any gardener. As is, *two* minutes for the allée.

Adding up, I find that the gardens of Towerhill Cottage (the plural sounds more substantial, somehow) are at this stage able to offer even the most languid visitor only twenty-seven minutes of viewing interest. This clearly falls short. Of course, I might have included the pheasants (where great estates have peacocks, we have pheasants strutting on the lawn, all hoping to evade the guns of November) a tremendous, nay sensational, bed of stinging nettles, and a similar stand of cow-parsley; the vegetable garden, cynosure of every rabbit's eye; the clearing in the wood just behind the vegetable garden that may one day be made to resemble one of the 'garden rooms' of our distinguished gardening neighbour Sir Roy Strong but just now contains one small oak tree, three larch stumps, an azalea ('Hino-Mayo') and a precious bit of mountain laurel; or the sunken garden, as yet little more than a construction site involving heaps of sand, crushed stone, pegs and string, unlaid flagstones, half built retaining walls and wild hopes. The herbaceous border mentioned above will eventually be incorporated into the sunken garden assuming all goes well.

So I must face the fact that we are still thirteen minutes of 'garden interest' shy of inclusion in the National Gardens Scheme. This is a troubling admission. It would be nice to believe our neighbour Roger Pemberton (whose extremely beautiful garden has, quite rightly, made it for the first time this year) when he claims to have heard that thirty minutes will do the trick, but I don't dare. Nor am I prepared to hire a gardener to close the gap, even though you can dig, mow, plant, prune, build, weed, clip and mulch only so much in a weekend. That would be cheating. Perhaps the best thing is to sit tight and let things grow. The 'interest' may grow too. And if it doesn't, well, I'm not sure I really want visitors anyway.

The Blown Rose

If anything can be called a universal flower, it's probably the rose. Yet the English have some justice on their side when they claim it for their very own. The rose is England's national flower, the English climate is tailor-made for growing them, and English poets would be quite lost without roses to fuel their metaphors. A recent survey suggests that four out of five English gardeners grow roses, and no fewer than 2,000 varieties are available for sale here (more, probably), ranging from the terrifying 'Kiftsgate' (*Rosa filipes* 'Kiftsgate') – the original one is now 100 feet wide, 50 feet high and in excellent health and spirits – to the diminutive Cinderella, which can produce buttonholes for a Barbie doll.

All the more painful to report, therefore, that roses are having a very bad time of it over here just now. I am referring not to the incidence of black spot or aphids (those are pretty bad too) but to an event that shook the English rosarian community to its roots last summer. Declaring that he was finally fed up with tending his roses, the distinguished gardener Christopher Lloyd ripped them out bodily, keeping only seven plants out of the hundreds that had occupied the beds since his father Nathaniel and Sir Edwin Lutyens first laid out the grounds of Great Dixter ninety years ago. Anyone familiar with Lloyd's classic *The Well-*

Tempered Garden, first published in 1970, won't be too surprised. He has never hidden his feelings about roses, viewing their gangly habit, off-season awkwardness and general vulnerability with an exceedingly cold eye. 'If we can't grow decent roses without spraying them a dozen or more times through the growing season, then the answer is to grow something else,' he grumbled back then. The writing was already on the garden wall. You only wonder what took him so long to read it. In place of the roses Great Dixter now boasts an array of exotics and other profoundly non-rose substitutes – hardy banana plants, lavender-blue *Verbena bonariensis*, purple cannas and castor-oil plants. The effect is very fine, if unsettling to the conservatives.

While it hardly spells the end of the English Rose, Lloyd's act has a certain symbolic significance. Roses have indeed been losing favour gradually in Great Britain. One unofficial estimate puts the decline over the past fifteen years at more than 60 per cent, with the total number grown now only about 20 million. That is, admittedly, still a lot of roses. But it is clear which way the wind is blowing.

I'm no expert on roses, heaven knows. If I were, I might be less startled by the number of ills these lovely things are heir to. Among them are virus diseases, mildew, aphids, leafhoppers, scale insects, red spiders and grubs. If a chafer bug doesn't get it, a leaf-cutter bee will. Then there is the general loss of vigour in choice varieties, occurring for genetic reasons or because they are on the wrong rootstocks. To say nothing of a terrible tendency to suckering, which must be answered by something approaching violence ('Cutting them off is worse than useless: they must be torn off below ground where they leave the root,' as Hugh Johnson puts it delicately).

It's all enough to make even David Austin despair. Roses are also prey, it seems, to a sort of tired-soil syndrome, which makes them droop and fail if planted in the same place that a rose grew previously. If you treat one especially well – say, by tucking it in comfortably with a large serving of manure – then it will more than likely produce quantities of soft growth particularly suscept-ible to rust. Pruning is another problem. All the books say you must do it carefully and knowledgeably if you are to get your quota of blooms.

Worst of all – or at least most prevalent of all – is black spot. This affliction has apparently been getting worse ever since 1836, when *Rosa foetida*, a bright-yellow variety, arrived in Eng-land from Persia. Before that, a good yellow rose was a rare thing here, but black spot was too because varieties then avail-able tended to be resistant. (The oriental *R. bracteata*, the 'Macartney rose' brought from China in 1793, is actually almost immune, being generally indestructible; see p. 27.) Also the successful effort to improve air quality by reducing the emission of sulphur and other pollutants, which has been going on for much of this century, has made matters even worse. While breath-ing less junk makes us humans feel better, cleaner air also seems to have made life much easier for *Diplocarpon rosae*. There has, incidentally, been a flap lately about whether or not you are supposed to pick up and dispose of dead leaves from under your rosebushes, so as to prevent black-spot spores from develop-ing. The definitive *New RHS Dictionary of Gardening* says, curi-ously enough, that the spores develop on dead leaves in the United States but not in Britain. Why this should be is a mystery. Disbelieving British gardeners – encouraged by the Royal National Rose Society – are still picking up the leaves and burning them, just in case.

Anything else? Well, in the current mood of absolute candour about roses, some people are even complaining about the way they look. Most famously this year Sir Simon Hornby, the new president of the Royal Horticultural Society, was quoted as saying, 'I hate rose gardens. I never know why people have them – they don't have weigela gardens or philadelphus gardens. A formal rose garden is as ugly a thing as you can find.' Sir Simon has been chairman of W. H. Smith, Britain's largest chain of bookstores, a fact which made one gardening writer wonder how it could be, given the artistic level of some of his merchandise, that the gentleman had never seen anything uglier than a formal rose bed.

A formal rose bed is plainly an acquired taste, and one less common than it used to be. When the bushes are without blooms, and spaced out with mathematical precision in a box-framed expanse of carefully raked, absolutely bare soil, they possess a kind of scratchy elegance that could easily pass for ugliness. But it doesn't have to. I saw a planting like that the other day, laid out inside the immaculately kept confines of the walled courtyard of a Queen Anne house in the Herefordshire countryside; against the mellow red brick it had the sparse and angular charm of an etching. Granted that most of us prefer lithographs, if not something yet more perfervid, I'm willing to acknowledge that austerity in the garden has its place.

A formal rose bed off-bloom is probably the real nadir anyway. As the gardening writer Richard Bisgrove has observed, the most refined varieties of (non-shrub) roses are 'essentially beautiful flowers on rather ugly sticks', and it is the flowers rather than the sticks that we're after. Mixing roses with other plants in a border, or letting them climb into trees, or shifting to older, less finicky varieties – these are the ways forward. After the holocaust at Great Dixter, Christopher Lloyd argued that he wasn't really against roses, but against the way roses are mishandled and grown for the wrong reasons, such as snob appeal ('Those with the greatest snob value tend to have French or historical names, associated with a whiff of stale potpourri') or 'satisfaction of the knockout, gorblimey kind for sheer size and brilliance'. He believes that a rose ought to 'be able to cope with the hurly burly of border life'. William Robinson, incidentally, was saying the same thing 100 years ago: 'There is a great loss to the flower garden from the usual way of growing the rose as a thing apart.'

In the minds of most Englishmen, the ideal 'rose as a thing apart' is the Hybrid Tea; Hybrid Teas are still by far the most popular roses bought and grown in Britain. Three Hybrid Teas are sold for every Floribunda. In the list of the ten bestselling roses of 1992, seven were HTs, and so were the top two. The most popular of all was a handsome copper-coloured Hybrid Tea called (sorry) Just Joey, which has been heading the charts ever since they started keeping track in 1983. For producing perfect blooms, Hybrid Teas are unmatched, and they also come in just about every colour you can think of. (Except blue. The blue rose has always eluded geneticists, though there is now hope, if that's the word. Australian scientists – backed by the Japanese distiller Suntory – say soberly that they have just succeeded in snipping the key blueness genes out of petunias and yeast and inserting them into roses. 'The Japanese and the Americans seem most excited,' a spokesman reported blandly.)

While I'm not about to get mixed up with Hybrid Teas, blue or otherwise, I do feel a certain responsibility to grow roses in Skenfrith. This is the home, after all, of the original red rose of Lancaster, *Rosa gallica* var. *officinalis*, which, according to legend, was found growing wild near the Lancastrian castle of Grosmont, our neighbouring village, in the fourteenth century. Admittedly, the wild roses I find these days in the woods and the hedgerows aren't red but a rather depressing white, and, when allowed to go unclipped, race upward to produce tremendous lacerating stems 30 feet long and an inch thick.

Our garden roses are more agreeable, growing not in bare and exclusive rose beds but a variety of less official places. There is a long-suffering but brave Albertine, dug up and divided by accident, that survived to put on an admirable display along a fence this summer and late into the autumn. (A cutting is showing all of its parent's vigour.) We have a couple of nameless gnarled shrubs settling into a new herbaceous border with a minimum amount of fuss. We have a simple white Cécile Brünner in a pretty bush, now threatening to get out of hand, that covers itself beautifully in hips each winter, and persists in sending up water shoots like rockets when we aren't looking. There's a creamy-flowered Albéric Barbier, fragrant with the scent of Rhine wine, growing vigorously in a swirl along the ground and up a stake as it waits for the pergola it has been promised. And there are others – a brilliant red Dublin Bay on the vegetable garden fence, a Golden Showers climbing an old stone wall, a rich white Iceberg set off beautifully by the black clapboarding of the barn. Nothing fancy.

Judging from our experience, I figure roses are here to stay. What else is so sweetly scented, and so pleasant to the eye, and so much fun to fool around with? What else can give you such splendid bloom in the dog days? Not (with all due respect) an 8-foot-tall castor-oil plant. And while roses *can* be a fiddle, they will also survive nonchalance on the gardener's part. Not long ago one of the many British television gardening programmes ran an experiment in pruning roses, which is, as we all know, a delicate and sophisticated enterprise. One bush was shaped by an expert with secateurs. The other was rudely dismasted with an electric hedge clipper. They then showed us what the bushes looked like a year later. You couldn't tell the difference.

Taste

England is so full of great gardens that it's hard for the poor tourist to know where to start, but even so there's something special about Sissinghurst. According to the latest statistics, the gardens created there by Vita Sackville-West and her husband Harold Nicolson starting sixty years ago draw 150,000 people a year, and at least another 50,000 would turn up if the National Trust, which owns the place, felt there was room. Things are so bad (or good, depending on your perspective) that you may have to book a time in advance in order to get through the gate on a busy weekend or run the risk of a fruitless wait in the car park.

There are several theories about why Sissinghurst is so popular. The most obvious is that the gardens are indeed very beautiful. They are also relatively small – perhaps 7 acres in all if you don't go out into the meadows – and can be viewed comfortably in an hour or two. But there is another reason for Sissinghurst's appeal, one that has practically nothing to do with gardening. The Nicolsons, gone these many years – she died in 1962, he in 1968 – seem to have achieved the kind of star status they never had when they were alive. They were literary, with connections to Bloomsbury; they had a bizarre marriage (described by their son Nigel in his bestselling book – later televised – *Portrait of a*

Marriage); and they were desperately upper-class in a way that Americans would like to think is typical here but isn't. Part of the charm of Sissinghurst, therefore, is the fact that it is not only a great and elegant garden, but the essence of English aristocratic taste (and, if you will, decadence). At the cost of a day trip from London, you get the garden and the fantasy both.

I'm not about to suggest even in passing that Sissinghurst is less than a complete success, on its own terms or any other; its excellences have stimulated imitations in hundreds of lesser gardens. Vita's White Garden, for instance, a square, yew-hedged enclosure filled entirely with white, cream and silver-grey blossoms and foliage, patterned with low box and centred on a dazzling bower of white rose *longicuspis*, has generated as much praise as anything since the aerial plantings of Babylon. Then there is Harold's Lime Walk, brilliant with tiny spring bulbs that require incessant weeding, and drifts of narcissi beneath the flowering cherries of the Orchard. In autumn a long narrow border of blue *Aster frikartii* 'Mönch' glows along the ancient brick wall Vita discovered and excavated; in midsummer there is the rose bed embracing a rondel of high yew hedges. Moreover, the whole ensemble is indisputably tasteful. A host of gardening writers have said so, and heaven knows that Vita and Harold would have been the first to agree.

This fact was driven home the other day by the publication of a book called *The Decline and Fall of the British Aristocracy* by the historian David Cannadine, in which he devotes a fairly destructive chapter to the Nicolsons. In his view, they were snobs, and even their choice of garden plants showed it. 'Any flowers remotely tinted with the middle class or the suburbs were ruthlessly excluded,' he writes. 'Azaleas were unsuitable because they were "Ascot, Sunningdale sort of plants", rhododendrons were like "fat stockbrokers, who we do not want to have to dinner".' Although a few defenders sprang to with letters to *The Times* (pointing out, for example, that Sissinghurst boasts a handsome collection of azaleas), Cannadine was dead right about the Nicolsons' sense of horticultural discrimination. 'You with your extraordinary taste,' Harold wrote to Via in June 1937, 'have made it look like nobody's garden but your own. I think the secret of your gardening is simply that you have the courage to abolish ugly or unsuccessful flowers.'

As a rule of thumb, that's not bad, though it reminds me slightly of the argument that the way to success in publishing is to publish nothing but big bestsellers. After all, one man's ugly flower is another man's pride. Who's to say who is right? This is where 'taste' is invoked to settle the debate.

Some people might at this point waffle about how taste is relative too, but not the gardening writer Christopher Lloyd. He leaves no doubt about *his* position: 'I believe there are absolute standards of what goes and what doesn't in matters of taste.' Lloyd himself has never been reluctant to let us know what, so far as he is concerned, 'doesn't go'. Listen to him on *Polygonum affine* 'Donald Lowndes': 'I loathe it . . . how can it be so handsome and effective and yet, basically, such a horrid plant? . . . not just coarse; it is coarse-grained to its innermost fibre.' (*Polygonum*, anyone?) Or on those poor souls who lack a sensitivity to colour: 'Colour addicts who lurch incontinently from lumps of forsythia and double pink "Kanzan" cherries, through a blaze of rhododendrons and dumpy blobs of azaleas, floribunda roses, scarlet salvias, and so to a dying exit with mop-headed chrysanthemums.'

At one time or another, most gardeners – and especially gardening writers – express their disdain for certain plants. (Even Harold Nicolson once complained jokingly that 'Vita only likes flowers which are brown and difficult to grow.') The implied ground for dismissal is usually taste, but you don't have to look very far to see that the poor outcasts of our gardens have offended for a variety of reasons. They may be tricky to raise or (as in the case of the Nicolsons) be associated with the wrong sort of people. They may have been irredeemably misused in the past, like Victorian bedding plants, or simply overbred to a state of banality, like a salmon-coloured delphinium. They may, in fact, be ugly – my opinion of a droopy amaranthus.

What strikes me as remarkable, however, is the unanimity of opinion about just which plants are unacceptable. Floribunda roses, for example, have been widely attacked in recent years, not only for their unattractiveness out of season but also for the unsettling quality of their blooms. In the opinion of Katherine White, author of *Onward and Upward in the Garden*, 'Even a small vaseful of Peace roses is grotesque.' A whole range of bedding plants – petunias, cannas, geraniums, wax begonias, lobelias, calceolarias, celosias, kniphofias (Harold Nicolson speaks of 'those beastly red-hot pokers') – seems to have fallen beyond the pale. The best people simply don't grow gladioli or mop-headed hydrangeas or fastigiate flowering cherries. Dahlias, especially the huge peony-flowered kind developed by ambitious breeders and never otherwise seen on earth, come in for plenty of criticism (the great English gardener E. A. Bowles, seeing some 'magnificently grown' ones, could not resist asking the grower, 'in as innocent a tone as I could manage', whether he fried or steamed them). Serious garden buffs in Britain look down on the common *Rhododendron ponticum*, the mauve kind that grows wild over here, for its 'vulgar' colour, and I have the distinct impression that unless you possess a deep glade with room for a couple of hundred huge bushes, you'd better be careful about introducing any other kind of rhododendron either. A particular repugnance attaches to shrubbery with yellow or variegated leaves. (They can be 'extremely vulgar', according to Sir Simon Hornby, the president of the Royal Horticultural Society, who is prepared to be supernally critical. 'God's palette of flowers is absolutely wonderful, but when he got to variegation he sometimes went astray.') Golden privet also falls into this black hole, as does spotted laurel, apparently doomed for appearing too commonly in Edwardian front gardens.

For several years now, the *Guardian* newspaper has been running a series of articles proposing the 'best' and 'worst' of the twentieth century (the best restaurateur, the best literary biography, and so on), inviting readers to challenge their choices. A recent subject was the worst botanical creation. After saying rude things about a tulip called 'Ringo', a double sunflower (*Helianthus* 'Orange Sun') – 'like a grotesque stunted apricot floormop' – and *Rudbeckia occidentalis* 'Green Wizard', 'which actually has no petals at all and apparently lasts forever in that desperate condition', the *Guardian* came down hard on what is widely regarded as the leading horticultural horror of the century. This is the Leyland cypress, × *Cupressocyparis leylandii*, whose principal talent seems to be an ability to grow *fast*. Unattractive as a specimen tree ('it droops as if perpetually drenched by Manchester rain'), *leylandii* is usually planted as a hedge. In this form it can put on 3 feet a year if not subdued by frequent clipping, ultimately reaching 100 feet or so and darkening whole neighbourhoods. Hugh Johnson, author of *The Principles of Gardening* and an exceptionally knowledgeable tree man, gloomily writes: 'Fifty years hence, when all the millions recently planted are full-grown, Britain will be unrecognizable.'

Taste in plants can change, of course, and indeed does. Topiary, for example, is perfectly acceptable now. The ancient carved yew hedges at Levens Hall in Cumbria attract great admiration, and clipped birds and animals strut across lawns from the Cots-

wolds to Maryland. Yet 100 years ago William Robinson abomi-
nated topiary ('What right have we to deform things given us so
perfect and lovely in form?'), and Alexander Pope made wonderful fun of it in the early eighteenth century with his mock
'Catalogue of Greens' ('Adam and Eve in yew; Adam a little
shattered by the fall of the Tree of Knowledge in the great
Storm; Eve and the Serpent very flourishing . . . St George in
Box; his arm scarce long enough, but will be in a condition to
stick the Dragon by next April . . .'). Whether time will restore
leylandii to favour remains to be seen, but it is already clear that
taste is by no means eternal.

In this respect, as in so many others, Gertrude Jekyll may
offer us a good lesson. Unlike Vita (who did not wholly approve
of Gertrude's gardening theories, dismissing herbaceous-border
plants *en masse* as 'coarse things with no delicacy or quality
about them'), Miss Jekyll was willing to put up with nearly
every growing thing – scarlet salvias and red celosias and even
gladioli – provided they were grown in the right company. With
her, taste was less a matter of exclusion than of understanding.
'A geranium was a geranium long before it was a bedding plant,'
she pointed out, and was inclined to find good in the most
maligned inhabitants of the garden. 'She speaks as tenderly of a
deformed pear,' Betty Massingham notes in her biography of
Jekyll, 'as she might of some crippled child. "One is so sorry",
she says, "for a poor fruit."'

I have to admire this attitude. In spite of the beauty of Sissinghurst, there is something slightly unnerving about the Nicolsons'
certainty that they were more right than the rest of us. On the
other hand, my own taste being as sound as it is, I know I'm
right about that amaranthus.

Mole Wars

On the whole, I get along pretty well with the other creatures in and around the garden. There seem to be fewer of them on this side of the Atlantic than there are in New England or, at any rate, fewer aggressive ones. Reading Roger Swain's account in *Horticulture* a few months back of his trials with deer, raccoons, moose, woodchucks, foxes, rabbits and heaven knows what else, it struck me how lucky I am. While it's true that deer are beginning to come back to my neighbourhood, drifting westward out of the Forest of Dean, that the foxes never left (what would the Monmouthshire Hunt do without them?) and that I still don't trust the ubiquitous pheasants, there's only one beast that really gets my goat. It's the mole.

Before coming to England a few years ago, I never took moles very seriously. The only mole I'd ever seen was one the cat brought in, and, to be honest, it may have been a vole; when the cat finished with it there were, as they say, few identifying marks. If anybody asked, I suppose I would have ranked the mole as a garden menace somewhere around the level of summer lightning. Compared to the destructive capacity of a family of deer, ready and willing to eat anything from a prized candytuft border to a half-grown sugar maple, a mole seemed like a frail nonentity scarcely worth bothering about.

I now know better, much better. All by itself, a mole can make hash out of a half-acre lawn or give a meadow a case of giant measles. In Britain the big mechanical diggers used to excavate skyscraper foundations and opencast coal mines are known as JCBs. A mole is a worm-powered JCB. You have to see it to believe it, and even then you might be sceptical.

Let me be specific. A molehill (forget what you've been taught about its insignificance compared with a mountain) is, on average, 4 inches high and 8 inches in diameter. It is a substantial pile of earth, loose at first but gradually subsiding under the influence of rain into a solid lump that is lethal to any sprig of turf unfortunate enough to be trapped under it. Hit one with a mowing machine and you'll know it; hit two or three and it's off to the repair shop.

Technically, of course, a molehill is nothing more than a spoil heap shoved up by an extremely hard-working tunneller who has to put the dirt *some place*. He doesn't do it to annoy. In fact, he has another tunnelling method that does not produce molehills, in which he merely squirms along just under the surface of the ground, leaving raised ridges. This might sound harmless, until you step on a ridge and sink ankle-deep into the hollow air space below. There's no need to go into the other depressing aspects of mole engineering, such as the 'fortresses' they are said to erect sometimes, gargantuan molehills containing a network of tunnels and nests. I'm glad to say that I have never seen one of these.

My negative feelings about moles have apparently been shared by a great many Britons, both now and in the past. Much has been written about them, very little of it either complimentary or affectionate. True, after William III's horse tripped over a molehill and killed him in 1702, William's Jacobite enemies made a point of toasting 'the little gentleman in black velvet'.

And, as I remember it. Mole in *The Wind in the Willows* is presented as a companionable fellow. But in general when people think of moles they think mostly about how to get rid of them.

Traditionally, we had professional mole catchers. Until quite recently there was a good market for mole skins; the delicate and attractively coloured fur was used to make coats. In 1900 a single 3½-by-2½-inch pelt could bring as much as three shillings and sixpence, a day's wages for a labouring man. Every village had a couple of codgers equipped with spades and a fund of patience. In some areas you can still hire a mole killer, a sort of rural exterminator licensed to poison moles with strychnine-laced worms, but it's an expensive business. My neighbour had 10 acres of sheep-run cleared by a professional last year, only to see the critters come back with the cool weather in the autumn. It seems that there are always new moles hanging around in the woods and hedgerows waiting to repopulate abandoned tunnels. It takes only a few moles to accomplish an incredible amount of earth-moving.

I discovered this fact while reading up on moles (know your enemy). I also found out the following:

• A mole can travel up to 2½ miles through a tunnel. One has been observed to chase – and *catch* – a frog.

• The protuberant nose of a mole is extremely sensitive, and he is virtually blind. He presumably navigates by smell and feel. However, Kenneth Mellanby, author of *The Mole*, remarks despairingly, 'We do not really know how a mole finds its way about.'

• Moles eat only meat – mainly worms – although gourmet moles have been known to gnaw on truffles. Normal mole habitat has plenty of worms, and gardeners need not worry about their stock being depleted.

• Moles are extremely bad-tempered. Put two moles together and they will try to kill each other, frequently succeeding. Under the circumstances it is difficult to see how they manage to mate, but given the number of moles extant, they have obviously figured out some way.

• Being so quarrelsome and solitary, a single mole tends to occupy a large territory. Four or fewer to the acre is the average density. This means my lawn is host to (read victim of) no more than one or two moles, which may be reason for hope.

• A lone mole can shove as much as 10 pounds of soil – fifty times its own weight – up into molehills in the space of twenty minutes. This is equivalent to a coal miner lifting 12 tons an hour all by himself. (The average, with machinery, is 1 ton an hour.)

Out of raw necessity, gardeners spend a good bit of time exchanging anti-mole tactics. The first one I heard about sounded authentic enough because of its source. An old farmer just up the road claimed to know that moles emerged from their burrows precisely at 4.30 every afternoon. If you had a gun and sneaked up on them, you could dispatch them before teatime. Our resident thirteen-year-old took up the challenge, but an hour sitting paralysed in a deckchair in the middle of the meadow, armed with an air rifle, ended in no moles and permanent disillusionment with old farmers.

When the moles began moving into my lawn, I realized that stronger measures were called for. I turned to mole smokes. These are cardboard cylinders resembling shotgun shells, only bigger, with a twist of blue paper at one end and a filling of noxious chemicals. To use one, you dig under a fresh molehill until you locate the run, a horizontal tunnel that, as a rule, is about 3 or 4 inches down. (This may sound straightforward enough; in wet red clay, it isn't.) Then you unfurl the blue paper, light it with a match – making sure to stay upwind – and, when the smoke begins to billow, shove the cylinder into the run, sealing the whole affair with a chunk of sod. The fumes circulate through the run, making it inhospitable (possibly deadly) to the moles. That is the theory, anyway. There can, however, be problems. It's easy to extinguish the mole smoke inadvertently as you insert it – 75 pence up in smoke or, rather, *not* up in smoke. Or the tunnel may have collapsed or been blocked. Or your mole may have already departed for pastures new. Or perhaps he enjoys the smell. Still, for four or five years now a couple of dozen timely mole smokes have kept my lawn moderately pustule-free.

This winter the mole wars escalated. The crisis arose when the local hardware merchant reported that the company making my brand of mole smokes had gone out of business. The only kind now available costs more than twice the price. Much as I dislike moles, I'm not prepared to lay out *that* kind of money in chasing them off my patch, especially if, as seems likely, there are only two of them. So I have been collecting other ideas, spurred on by a report in the *Daily Telegraph* about the adventures of John Hampton, of Kent.

Mr Hampton, in a fit of gloom, ran an advertisement offering to pay 'almost anything' for a surefire way to rid his lawn of moles. He had, he said, tried smoke bombs, creosote, traps and toy windmills. None worked.

In terms of volume, the response to Mr Hampton's ad was encouraging, though some people inexplicably took it as a joke. Others didn't. Their suggestions included having a lawn party, with dancing; burying a milk bottle to convey above-ground sounds into the runs; flooding the runs with water and whacking the moles with a mallet as they emerged; hooking up a garden hose to a car exhaust and gassing them underground; treating the lawn with liquid worm-killer, thus depriving the moles of dinner; pouring bleach or similar substances down the hole; planting caper spurge (*Euphorbia lathyrus*), which moles are reputed to abhor but, according to Mellanby, don't; and placing a long-running, battery-operated Taiwanese noise-maker in the tunnel.

Hampton finally came up with his own solution. He took a tank of liquid butane from his barbecue and let it fizz into a mole hole for ten minutes or so. He hasn't see a molehill since. I feel for his neighbours.

So far as I am concerned, I have a hunch that the battle is just beginning. I've already tried a few classic strategies – a handful of mothballs down a hole, for example – to no avail. I don't have much faith in traps, but I mean to get one.

In the meantime I have come upon what must be the most elegant anti-mole weapon yet. In his Christmas round-robin newsletter last year the distinguished British chemist Frederick Dainton commented that Wrigley's Juicy Fruit chewing-gum apparently possesses an irresistible pheromonic appeal for male moles. All you need to do is put a stick of it down the hole. The mole, as Lord Dainton puts it, 'fails to appreciate that its internal bodily fluids and this gum are the essential ingredients of a new composite material of unparalleled rigidity'.

Talk about stiffing a mole.

Stone

Last week I put the last capstone on the transverse wall. It isn't the end of my Great Stonework Project, but the whole thing has some shape now; if you squint, you can almost imagine that it's finished. An incentive to completion was the final 3 tons of walling stone I managed to bring home from a field on the outskirts of Monmouth. It almost put paid to the trailer I borrowed from my neighbour Alan Jones, even though I kept the size of each load to 1,000 pounds or so. Stone is heavy stuff, and you need an amazing amount of it.

That's only one of the things I've learned in the course of this enterprise, which has been to build a sunken garden. Another is a powerful respect for cement. My ignorance is not nearly as profound as it was when I started, but I have a sneaking feeling that I missed more than one trick along the way. Local builders and DIY books did help, but if you have any suggestions, please feel free. It won't be the last stonework I undertake.

This is stone country. There are plenty of trees, but pretty much everything is built of stone, or was until cement blocks came along. Climate may have something to do with it, or the fact that stone has always been available for the digging in these hills. Carpenters can frame a window or a roof, but you get the distinct impression that they'd be happier avoiding wood, which won't last for 500 years. By the same token, when it came time to decide how to construct the retaining walls, steps and other features of our new garden I never for a moment considered using the railway sleepers that I would have used in the States. It had to be stone.

Towerhill Cottage sits on a highly irregular piece of ground, topographically speaking. The house itself burrows 2 or 3 feet below ground zero on the north side, while on the south side the hill slopes away toward the valley of the Monnow. As best I can figure it, a great many years ago an old-fashioned Welsh 'long house' stood on the site, with one end consisting of a barn. When the human end was replaced in the 1830s, the barn was not, and this — when it finally vanished — left a rectangular foundation-like depression, perhaps 18 by 25 feet, immediately to the west of the present house. For some years we have been gazing at this depression and bemoaning the hard-to-mow bank on one side of it. But then we suddenly realized that what we had here was the makings of a serious piece of garden architecture.

The plan went like this. We would cut the bank back to vertical, build a 3-foot-high retaining wall to hold it and put a nicely sheltered new bed along its base. (A raised bed already existed on the opposite flank of the depression.) Then we would construct a transverse retaining wall across the far end of the depression and create a raised platform for a pergola beyond it. The depression itself would be flagged with stone, while stone steps would give access to the platform. A new set of French doors in the side of the house would lead out into this pleasance.

The scheme sounded reasonably straightforward, and no doubt would have been if I'd been willing to pay a contractor to build the whole thing. In the event, I did get Brian Nash to come around with his backhoe to do the digging. The man is an artist. In the space of three hours he had cut back the bank, stripped the topsoil and piled it carefully, dug out the new bed 18 inches deep, 6 feet wide, and 20 feet long, levelled everything to the inch, and shoved about 20 tons of spoil out of the way in the wood where you couldn't see it. He also managed to get his gigantic machine out on to the road again without tearing down the gate.

At this point, I thought that the only problem presented by stone was getting enough of it. In our part of the Welsh Marches, the universal building stone is called Old Red Sandstone. It ranges from punky to very hard indeed, is predominantly though not universally reddish-brown in colour and was probably laid down between 350 million and 400 million years ago. As rocks go, Old Red is famous; some of the very first studies of fossils, made when the study of historical geology was in its infancy in the nineteenth century, dealt with insects and fish found in Old Red outcroppings. Around here, Old Red is the stone you find on the surface, blending with the deep burnt umber of the soil. Its virtues as a building stone include the fact that it splits horizontally fairly readily. Among its failings – as I will testify with imprecations, given half a chance – is its annoying reluctance to split without shattering in any other direction.

While there are plenty of small, abandoned quarries scattered around the neighbourhood, usually obscured by clumps of brambles and scrub, stone is not that easy to come by. I asked around. The local line seemed to be that if you wanted building stone, you bought a derelict barn. There are still a few to be found in outlying fields from the days before tractors. But while buying a barn may have been feasible up to a few years ago, stern countryside-planning regulations have queered that particular pitch. Although no *new* houses are allowed to be built, except in strictly controlled areas, you can generally get permission to convert an existing structure, no matter how decayed or ruinous it is. So a wrecked barn with a view is likely to turn up on the real-estate page priced at about £100 thou.

Then I heard about Perthir. In the fifteenth century, a large manor house had stood in a bend of the river about 3 miles east of us. By the eighteenth century, the house itself had been pulled down and the stones reused to build a range of barns and farm buildings nearby. Now Perthir was collapsing again. The farmhouse, inhabited by an elderly farmer and his wife, was sound enough, but the rest was mainly roofless, choked with charred beams, broken roof tiles, old farm implements, piles of manure and rotting bales of hay. Mrs Reece allowed as how they intended to bulldoze the whole lot into the ground if they couldn't sell the stone.

So for three icy winter days I methodically demolished a wall at Perthir, pulling stones out of a soft, thick mass of reddish plaster-mortar. The wall was extraordinarily thick, at least 4 feet, and the stones unquestionably old. Some showed signs of having been worked in ancient times, and there were a couple of definite finds: chunks of carved sandstone cusping from a Gothic window of the old manor house. When I had piled up what I thought was enough – about 5 tons, I figured – I got a friend with a tractor and trailer to help me take it back to Towerhill Cottage. (I paid Mrs Reece for 5 tons. This was regrettable, because a stone dealer later told me that I had actually secured about 2.)

A word here about classifying building stone. The best, called 'freestone', can be broken along any of three planes, producing a handsome chunk like an oversized brick. It is wonderful stuff, but rare. Old Red Sandstone, like most sedimentary stone, tends toward 'intermediate' – that is, more or less flat on top and bottom, with a flat third edge if you're lucky. In the old days masons would square off blocks of this with chisels. The third kind, 'non-freestone', is basically a shapeless (and hopeless) lump. The stone I had was intermediate, shading off into non-freestone.

I started on the long retaining wall in the dead of winter, which in Wales means mud and occasional ice, pegging out the line I meant to follow and stretching strings. Fortunately the earth the wall was intended to retain was firm, heavy clay, so I didn't need the help of temporary plywood sheets. In fact, that clay was so firm that I also ignored what the books said about digging a trench and pouring a concrete foundation. Instead, I laid down the biggest, flattest stones I could find, making a base for the wall about two-and-a-half feet wide. It is possible that I shall regret this in years to come.

It seems to me that a close-fitting dry-stone wall is more satisfying to look at than any other kind of wall, except possibly one made out of really old and mellow brick. Having consulted the authorities and examined the pictures of stone walls – especially those handsome hewn-stone affairs with joints so tight you can't stick the blade of a trowel into them – I knew what I wanted. Only one side of my wall would show, of course, so I could save the best stones for the outer face, jamming the irregular ones behind with dollops of mortar. The mortar I mixed out of sand and cement, three or four to one, with a slug of plasticizer in the water to keep the mix from drying out too fast. The latter tactic proved to be wise, because finding the right stone and fitting it in place often took ages.

I won't pretend that building the wall was a complete lark, but it did turn out to be addictive, like some physically challenging jigsaw puzzle. I'd heft a stone that appeared to be quite impossible, and discover that, after trying it out this way and that for five minutes or so, it would unexpectedly chunk into place. Still, as winter passed into spring and spring into summer, the plausible stones got fewer and fewer, and I began to realize why you don't see many dry-stone walls in our part of the country. That wall at Perthir had consisted of about two-thirds soft filler for very good reason: the only way to create a smooth-faced wall with stones like these is to sink them in plenty of mortar and stop pretending. That's what everyone in the neighbourhood has been doing for a thousand years or so.

By this time, however, I had built a lot of wall that looked for all the world like fitted, mortarless dry stone. I had kept all the mortar well back from the face, inside the structure, where it served to hold things together and keep the pretty part from falling down. To finish the way I had begun was shaping up as a challenge. Besides, I found, you could sometimes successfully square off a near-block with a hammer and a wide chisel called a 'bolster', scoring it where you wanted it to break and then delivering an almighty whack. If you didn't get a pile of rubble (and you often did), you might get another usable stone. In cases of real desperation, there was the angle grinder, a lethal tool consisting of a powerful electric motor turning a 9-inch abrasive disk at a deafening, terrifying speed. You held the thing – tightly – by two handles, pressed the trigger to bring it to life, and applied the edge of the disk to the stone. The immediate result was a blinding cloud of stone dust, a still louder noise, a horrible smell and a neat ¼-inch-deep cut across the stone, which could then, with luck, be broken with the bolster and hammer.

By such devices I gradually used up all the stone I had. Five more tons came from a dealer in Hereford at a stiff price (the advantage of this was delivery; I didn't bargain on the fact that the delivery would be made in the middle of the road) and still more from the man on the outskirts of Monmouth, who graciously threw in three stone troughs and a broken quern. The last lot happily contained some nicely squared pieces. You get so that nothing pleases the eye quite like a right angle.

It has now been roughly forty weekends since I pegged out the first wall. That wall is finished; so is the transverse wall, both of them capped with flagstones from the collection I managed to locate and buy, which is now stacked like a deck of gargantuan playing cards at the far side of the garden. The flags, I regret to say, are not Old Red; sandstone flags almost always break when you lift them and are unobtainable now. But they're the next best thing, blue-grey Pennant stone from old quarries near Bristol, removed from demolished cottages in the Welsh coal valleys. My walls, all 50 or so feet of them, are convincingly dry-stone (if you don't look too closely), complete with inadvertent bulges that I at least can live with. (According to the Japanese, perfection is impious.) It seems to me I'm right to be proud of them.

Now that the weather is cooler again and the midges have departed, I'm about to start laying the flagstones on the main part of the garden. These will be bedded in sand and levelled, but not cemented; it's okay if plants decide to spring up between them (and they will). Then I must build a set of shallow semi-circular steps leading up through an opening in the transverse wall to the platform where the pergola will be. The platform will be paved with broken flags, cemented in place (I am reluctantly forced to call this 'crazy-paving', for want of a less downmarket term). How the pergola will be constructed is still a matter of conjecture. I may try stone for the pillars – there is quite a lot left, of all shapes and sizes – but somehow at this point I rather favour wood.

Just to reassure you, in case you have gained the impression that what we've got here is not a garden at all, but something resembling a stoneyard, I should point out that in the intervals between mixing endless heaps of mortar and heaving rocks, I found time to fill — with a lovely mixture of the topsoil Brian saved and rotted sheep manure — the new bed at the foot of the wall. It is already occupied by a number of comfortable rose-bushes, potentillas, alchemillas, senecios, fuchsias and Johnson's blues. An Albertine has even begun clambering up the long retaining wall. On the coldest day it's pleasantly warm there. The afternoon sun seems to glow in the stone, and so it will, I hope, for the next few centuries now.

Asparagus

I've decided that anybody who succeeds in growing asparagus has a right to feel a twinge of self-satisfaction, if not downright triumph. It's tricky stuff. The best excuse for trying lies in the eating, of course. Plunged into briskly boiling water no more than thirty-five seconds after having been cut, coddled into barely drooping succulence and consumed with melted butter, there's nothing this side of ambrosia to match it. But to those of us curious about the *how* of growing things, as opposed to the *why*, asparagus has more to answer for. Short of undertaking to produce your own private bed of morels (and I noticed recently that somebody is trying to market a morel kit, heaven help us), it's hard to think of any vegetable enterprise less guaranteed to succeed than a brand-new asparagus bed.

Not everyone, I know, would agree with this gloomy assessment, and in fact it came as something of a surprise to me. A decade or so ago I planted an asparagus bed in the Berkshires without a great deal of fiddle, and it worked fine first time off, or rather mostly worked; those plants that didn't freeze during that first hard winter actually threw up a few thin spikes the next spring. Two or three subsequent years of mulching and weeding resulted in a crop significantly better than that produced by the single wild plant I had found growing under some lilacs next to the front door. It all seemed pretty straightforward. You dug a trench, you bought some two-year-old crowns, you plonked them into the trench and covered them as they grew. Then you waited patiently for a year or two and started eating.

A few years ago, transplanted to Britain and the owner of some fresh ground, I decided to try asparagus again. I had laid out my vegetable patch bordering a meadow in which sheep safely grazed, without realizing that in winter the meadow turned into one vast spring emitting water that flowed down a gentle slope straight into my new garden. In the autumn, unsuspecting, I dug my familiar 8-inch-deep asparagus trench on the upstream side. By the time the asparagus crowns arrived in the local garden centre in April, my trench looked like nothing so much as a miniature version of the Abergavenny–Brecon Canal. Planting asparagus in it was out of the question. By the time I managed to engineer a drainage ditch to carry some of the water away, the garden centre had sold out of asparagus crowns.

I like to think that I'm a person who learns from his mistakes. The next spring I was ready: new trench, drainage in place. The heavy red clay soil was, well, a bit *gummy* . . . but that couldn't be helped. Other things seemed to grow happily enough in that clay, and if I waited any longer for it to dry out, the crowns would be gone again. This time, out of fifteen crowns, one shoot came up. It looked very disconsolate and lonely, as well it might after struggling through 6 inches of near-ceramic to reach the light. Its fellows had apparently given up the ghost partway.

Then one lovely Sunday we happened to visit a grand house called Clytha. In addition to other horticultural wonders, Clytha has some splendid asparagus beds. They were exquisitely mulched and weed-free, long, raised mounds of friable black soil out of which poked stout stalks of asparagus like so many 75-mm anti-aircraft guns. It was at this point that I was forced to recognize that growing asparagus in the Welsh Marches, where frost seldom comes at all and, if it does, rarely penetrates more than an inch into the ground, may require a slightly different approach from that employed in the snowbound Berkshires. Imitating Clytha was the obvious solution. But how did they do it?

When faced with my own invincible ignorance, as a rule I fall back on books. In this case, I decided, the book had better be English. (There may be Welsh gardening books, but I never saw one, and couldn't read it if I had.) We were plainly dealing with un-American conditions. Fortunately the exact book was to hand – *The Domestic Gardener's Manual*, lengthily subtitled, by one John Towers, CMHS, MEAS, published in a Revised, Enlarged and Improved Edition in London in 1839. In addition to spelling out, in staggering detail, just about everything anybody could conceive of asking (and a lot that was inconceivable) about growing fruits and vegetables, Mr Towers had a fetching fondness for science. He was particularly possessed of the idea that electricity was the great secret of vegetative growth, noting that Darwin himself had suggested putting metal-topped stakes in the garden as a means of 'supplying plants more abundantly with the electric ether', and backing this up with his own observation of the tendency of plants to form 'pointed terminations' such as 'prickles and thorns' for electrical purposes. Towers also cherished the belief that 'the electric fluid' came from the 'decomposition' of the sun's rays within the surface of the earth.

Tempting as I found it to pursue this line of investigation, I really wanted to discover the secret of growing asparagus. I turned to 'Section II, Part I: The Natural History and Cultivation of Esculent Vegetables'. This began by retailing a number of odd asparagus facts. Did you know that, according to Pliny, the Romans produced asparagus near Ravenna so big that three stalks weighed a pound? That the steppes of Russia and Poland are covered with asparagus, which is eaten like grass by horses and oxen? That asparagus grown near London commanded the huge price of five shillings the hundred? (I didn't.) Then Towers proceeded to deal with what even I recognized as the key to asparagus success: preparing the bed.

Throughout his book, his method is to quote authorities. In this case he quoted several. The first advises trenching the ground to be planted to a depth of 2½ feet, 'burying plenty of dung in the bottom'. The second says to spread 10 inches of 'well-reduced horse dung' on the surface, and then dig it in 2 feet deep, digging a second time a few weeks later. The third explains that the way they do it in France is to dig a pit 5 feet deep as big as the intended bed, removing every stone 'even as low in size as a filbert nut', and filling this gigantic hole as follows: 6 inches of manure, 8 inches of turf, 6 more inches of manure, 6 inches of sifted earth, 8 inches of turf, 6 inches of very rotten dung, and 8 inches of the best earth. (Yes, I know that adds up to only 4 feet. Ask the French.) Finally, we hear from a Mr M'Phael (no doubt a colleague of Peter Rabbit's Mr MacGregor), who recommends double-digging a mixture of 'dung and vegetable mould' to a depth of 3½ feet, with 'the labourers standing and working in the bottom of the trench' in order to 'chop down the dung and earth together'.

That word 'labourers' is, of course, the giveaway. While I had an abundance of manure (we are surrounded by sheep), and turf too for that matter, labourers are in pretty short supply around Towerhill Cottage. There is, in fact, only one, me, and I was not about to spend the summer excavating and refilling a 5-foot (or even 3-foot) hole the size of a swimming pool. The author of *The Domestic Gardener's Manual*, to give him credit, does appear to recognize the problem because he goes on to describe a somewhat less majestic procedure he had tried out for himself in March of 1824. With what he called 'trifling exertions' he personally planted four 15-foot rows of two-year-old crowns in ground trenched and manured 'as deeply as possible', the trenching having been accomplished 'in a few hours' by a boy *with a wooden leg*!

For several reasons I found this a little hard to picture, but I couldn't argue with Towers's reported results – 700 spears in 1826, 1,100-plus in 1827, 1,292 in 1828. That's productivity (book-keeping too, for that matter). I was pleased to agree with his conclusion that no one should 'shrink from the attempt to obtain so fine a vegetable, through the fear of not being able to do it without a great deal of trouble'. I was not ready to shrink yet. I read farther.

Sand. That had to be the answer. 'Asparagus-ground should be light, yet rich; a sandy loam.' And again: 'M'Phael considers a deep mellow loam of a brownish colour . . . rather of a sandy than binding nature, as most propitious to the growth of asparagus.' So far as my soil was concerned, 'binding' was right on the mark, but I had a possible solution in the ten bags of sand left over from a recent construction project. I promptly dumped them on the garden and tilled them in. Admittedly, the depth was closer to 6 than 60 inches, but we do what we can. Anyway, the sand disappeared, as completely as if it had never existed. It must have done some good, because when planting time came the next spring the soil was slightly less sticky, and, in the heat of the following summer, a little less like an abandoned brickyard.

The next question was how deep to plant the crowns. As usual, Mr Towers's authorities lacked unanimity, apart from the fact that nobody so much as mentioned frost, but 2 inches below the surface seemed more or less right. The suggested distance apart also varied from 5 inches to 1½ feet, so I allowed 1 foot.

I soaked the crowns before planting them, and when I was done I spread some manure on top as a sort of vegetable snack. Sure enough, during the following weeks a whole lot of frail little stalks emerged. I let them branch out, as they will, into a cloud of light-green foliage, and in the autumn added them to the compost heap once they had turned brown and dry.

The second spring would be the test. As the early apple blossoms were breaking, and the new oak leaves reaching the size of a mouse's ear, the first spears duly appeared. There weren't many, and none that could be described as substantial (except for a couple of beauties that came up from that first row I had planted — and abandoned as a failure — the first time around). But gradually others in the new rows poked through the increasingly hard and discouraging-looking crust, their way eased in a few cases by deep cracks that developed as the clay dried out. I had asparagus: we actually ate some of it (it was delicious). But my bed, alas, was a far cry from Clytha. John Towers, CMHS, MEAS, would not have admired it.

These days it consists of two rows of roughly ten plants each, many of them alive. It is mostly weedless, but flat and bare, distinguished from the potato ground alongside mainly by a scattering of dried-out sheep manure. Then there are three or four plants from that first doomed row, mysteriously returned to life and now lurching skyward through a dense mixture of chives, quack grass and daisies in an inconvenient spot next to a fence.

I'm not quite sure what to do next. Roughly a third of the entire vegetable garden is already devoted to asparagus. The best thing might be to plough the lot under and start again, but there's something to be said for patience. Who knows what those feeble infants might become, provided they survive at all?

I keep looking at *The Domestic Gardener's Manual.* It's

seductive. Maybe, if I just dig another couple of rows, *seriously* dig them, I mean, going down 2½ feet and then dumping in plenty of manure, and mixing it with topsoil, and levelling it, and then setting out the crowns in precisely the right way, with the roots spread out flat and covered with just enough perfectly enriched soil to leave them buried 2 inches deep, and then digging straight alleys on either side of the bed, and spreading a little more loose soil over the bed, and beating the edges lightly with a spade so as to make the base a bit wider than the top, and then flooring the alleys with cinders, and raking the bed smooth, and in the autumn giving it a winter dressing of rotten manure and another 2-inch layer of fine soil, and then in the spring, in March, lightly forking the bed (with a proper three-pronged asparagus fork, used nearly horizontally so as not to damage the crowns) and raking off the excess soil, and doing all this faithfully for three years before cutting any spears – well, maybe I'll have an asparagus bed to be proud of. I'll let you know.

Gardening and Groundskeeping

'Gardening' is a dangerously imprecise term. By that I mean it covers too many activities, some of them mutually exclusive.

I'll explain. While we both call ourselves gardeners, because we both work in the garden from time to time, Carol and I have quite different approaches to the occupation. She is keen about plants. She can tell you which hebe is which. She knows how to take rose cuttings that thrive. She can tell you where to put a cistus so it doesn't get frosted and why pruning it won't work. A pretty authentic gardener, in fact, though she would insist that she has a lot to learn. I, on the other hand, am at heart a groundskeeper.

The depth of this distinction was forcibly brought home to me last summer when, in the course of clipping off the excess shoots underneath a clump of lilac, I carefully pruned a prized clematis so thoroughly to the ground that it vanished. It was not a *montana*, either, but a *jackmanii* that Carol had been gently urging into the lilac over the course of five years and was at last about to flower. Now you (and she) should understand that I didn't act the vandal on purpose. It's just that the lilac really needed cleaning up, and when you're crawling around on the ground one shoot may look pretty much like the next, to me at least. Unfortunately it did in this case.

It's all very well to say that these things happen, but they seem to happen to me more often than they should. In fact, they happen often enough to suggest that I should question my basic attitude towards vegetation. For example, I have always enjoyed using a string trimmer, in spite of its tendency to vibrate, smoke horribly and run out of string when the shops are closed. I even see myself as something of an artist with it, dashingly swooping within fractions of an inch of the daffodils in the lawn, circling around trees without damaging the bark, edging a path without spraying gravel in my face. (So the odd paperwhite falls victim, so there's a gouge or two along the path, so I happen to back into a nascent mallow and top it – you can't expect to be right *every* time.)

In any case, my point here is not the mistakes I make – everybody does that. The point is the degree to which I, as a typical groundskeeper, am drawn to gardening activities that are only marginally horticultural. Even when growing things are involved, I find myself tidying up. I'm responsible for the vegetable garden (largely because I like to cook and to eat, I suspect), but what I really enjoy is making the rows straight with a stretched string, keeping the beds weeded, and cultivating the soil to keep it loose – and nice to look at.

Mowing is probably the epitome of groundskeeping. I used to do all my own mowing, and probably still would except that I was prevailed upon to give employment to a husky fifteen-year-old from the village. I don't begrudge the ten quid – there's much to be said for having the job done before we arrive on Friday afternoon – and it gives me the opportunity to run lightly over the whole thing again, just polishing, as it were, and taking care of those corners and edges which only a fanatic cares about.

I'm glad to say that we also have some coarse mowing to be

done, which I tend to save for myself. One section is the orchard, amounting to a quarter of an acre or so, and the other the slightly larger open area sloping away from the house towards our view. Until early May, both of these sections contain wildflowers of varying impressiveness. The orchard has its early purple orchids, while the open slope has wild forget-me-nots, daffodils, violets, cow-parsley and a discouraging amount of dock. Mowing the orchard isn't a problem – you just leave the orchids to get on with it, rumbling over everything else with a big 22-inch mower that leaves the cut grass in neat windrows. Very satisfying. Mowing the slope is another matter.

This is where the groundskeeper and the gardener begin to show their true natures. The groundskeeper's instinct is to get out there and lay waste as soon as the grass has grown up to about 9 inches and the daffodils have passed their prime. The gardener demurs, noting how nice the slope looks in its spring green, studded with wildflowers. The groundskeeper protests that if we wait any longer, the mower won't cut it; it will have to be scythed. The gardener points out that the whole logic of gardening says we are supposed to enjoy growing things, not chopping them down. Why does everything have to be so neat anyway? At this juncture, the groundskeeper generally backs off and turns to something else, perhaps edging shrub beds with another of his favourite tools, the half-moon spade. Come July, he will finally manage to drive the mower through the grass and the cow-parsley, which is now 18 inches high. The effect will be of a very bad haircut. This pains him, but the wildflowers will have had their day in the sun.

Given his attitude, one might accuse the groundskeeper of actual hostility to growing things, but this is not fair. It's just that he is more sensitive than most to one of the great truths about plants. They are essentially aggressive. They want to win.

They want to beat out other, weaker, plants, and they want to beat out humans too. Left to their own devices, they will make a mockery of any garden. Brambles and bracken and wild roses will choke a wood, a hedgerow will turn into a narrow forest. In this contest I'm inclined to favour the human, which naturally calls for a certain amount of mowing, clipping and chopping.

As you may have gathered by this time, one theme defining the groundskeeper's role in the garden is destruction. Another is construction. By this I do not mean the execution of planting plans *à la* Gertrude Jekyll, those tempting hypothetical beds filled with labelled cloud or kidney shapes advising us where the hostas or the campanula or the hybrid phlox are supposed to go. (These always look better on paper, especially in books illustrated with exquisite watercolour paintings of the bed in full bloom. Hard to say why, but ours don't come out that way. Maybe – whisper it – the gardener doesn't know enough.) I'm talking about *real* construction – walls, steps, paving, pergolas, arbours, all sorts of engineering work from earth-moving to building nesting boxes.

Somehow these activities seem to conflict less with the concerns of the gardener. In fact, one might even note a certain commonality of interest. Our new summer garden, including stone walls, flagstones and a substantial pergola, took years (enjoyable years), and, thinking back, I realize that it was all the gardener's idea in the first place. She quite rightly recognized that roses would be grateful for the new bed, that the walls would shelter and warm the half-hardy perennials, and in the long run (i.e. when and if the sun came out some summer's day) it would be pleasant to have lunch under the canopy of foliage covering the pergola. Of course, the canopy of foliage is yet to develop, but that's the gardener's problem.

The latest scheme, which emerged only last weekend, had a

similar origin. The idea is to build a long rustic fence, 6 or 7 feet high, on which roses can be trained. This will run down one side of a rectangular lawn, properly dividing it from another lawn that is at present set off only by some dubious lilacs, a telephone pole, a wild plum tree and a group of self-seeded ashes. The gardener would love to plant a whole array of roses here – a couple of red Dublin Bay, a François Juranville or two, a Bobbie James – making, in effect, a wall of roses.

The groundskeeper is delighted. The job will mean, first, digging out all the lilacs. Then he will have to cut down at least two of the trees and excavate about a hundred daffodil bulbs. The rose bed itself will need to be prepared. Then will come the nicest part: going into the wood to find, cut and trim hundreds of feet of poles – ash and oak and larch, probably – with which to build the fence. It will take months of weekends, given the amount of mowing, hedge-clipping, string-trimming, edging, pruning and miscellaneous groundskeeping that has to be done at the same time.

In the meantime, gardening will go on – cuttings taken, new plants discussed and purchased, seeds planted and fertilized. There may even be some watering done, unlikely as that seems now in the rains of April. No doubt the groundskeeper will be called upon to help from time to time, digging planting holes, say, and possibly even contemplating where a rather peaked shrub might be moved to give it a better chance. His mind will naturally be occupied by other schemes – clearing a new section of the wood, for example, sawing up and splitting fallen trees for firewood, building that rose fence – but he is not entirely averse to horticulture in its purer sense, which might be regarded as fortunate. Any garden consisting of more than a window-box needs both approaches.

I'm happy to report that a perfect illustration of this

convergence of interests appeared last week. The *jackmanii* that the groundskeeper had so carelessly and completely clipped into oblivion last summer has emerged with hugely renewed vigour, sending half a dozen stems racing up into the lilac as if a year's quiet sojourn underground had been just what it wanted. I don't know about the gardener, but I feel better.

Compost

We are blessed (some, including me, would say cursed) with a curiously awkward kind of soil. It is decidedly red, almost entirely free of stones and heavy, heavy, heavy, a sort of half-melted terracotta. When it's wet, which is most of the time, it adheres to everything – wellington boots, shovels, rototiller tines, barrow wheels and your knees. When it's dry (briefly, in the summer or an extended drought), it hardens into chunks unbreakable by any tool short of a 14-pound sledgehammer or possibly a brick bolster. Yet it is wonderfully fertile stuff. Plants seem to love our soil, especially when it behaves in a cooperative spirit and doesn't strangle them at birth.

On the whole, therefore, I suppose we are luckier than some. Red clay holds water; it is at least potentially fertile; it has almost neutral pH; and if you could only work it more easily – in the vegetable patch most years there's not much chance of digging and achieving a normal tilth any earlier than late May – it would be a perfect garden medium. All it needs is a bit of easing up. In the past decade I've done my best to achieve this modest goal. Nobody could say I've succeeded, although there are places – generally spots in which my unknown predecessors obviously dug for centuries – where you can find something resembling loam.

One of the first things I tried was sand. This is very expensive, and for that reason alone impractical, but I had some of it to spare and at the time was obsessed with growing asparagus. I won't say it did the trick, but it didn't do any perceptible harm. I suppose it turned to clay.

Then there was gypsum. My friend at the local garden centre swore that an application of powdered gypsum was sure to break down the heaviest soil. In fact, he said, it was just the ticket for clay. So I bought a couple of pounds and dusted it thickly over a potato patch. Before I dug it in, it looked exactly like snow. I regret to say that so far as breaking the clay was concerned, it was precisely as effective as snow, too.

The Wormery was – perhaps still is – more promising. We got one for Christmas from a thoughtful relative. It consisted of a large green garbage can with a hinged lid and a small tap near the bottom. When it came, inside was a small cardboard box full of 'standard compost worms' (*Eisenia andrei* and *E. foetida*, if you want to get technical), an instruction book and a few other odds and ends.

We promptly set it up in the utility room next to the washing machine, and gave the worms their first feeding of kitchen debris – vegetable tops, peelings, spoiled fruit and whatnot. (The instruction book didn't baulk at meat scraps, but we did.) Sure enough, the stuff we put in began to disappear, silently and (thank heavens) odourlessly. For the first few weeks it was customary to find worms crawling up the inside walls of the can instead of burrowing the way they were supposed to; we even found a few desiccated escapees scattered on the floor when we arrived from the city on a Friday afternoon (I never did figure how they got out). But eventually they settled down, and things looked good on the fertility front.

So far, in the course of a year, I've used the handy tap to

draw off about a gallon and a half of brown liquid. The instruction book describes this as concentrated plant food, and, so far as I can see, it hasn't done my plants any harm. So far as soil conditioning is concerned, however, the jury is still out because I have not yet ventured to get the muck out of the bottom of the can. It's supposed to be terrific stuff, and if you do it right – skimming off and saving the top 5 inches or so, which contains the worms – you can recycle the wildlife. Of course, I've got no more than two or three bucketfuls in there, which cannot hope to convert much clay to loam (a little muck goes a short way).

Manure is another matter. We are surrounded, at Towerhill Cottage, by sheep. They graze in our meadow, they gambol through the fields across the lane and down the hill, they chorus mournfully each evening as Alan Jones arrives with their feed supplement. In lambing season, in the dead of winter, they produce manure, a lot of manure. (Of course, they produce it all year long, but in winter they're indoors, which concentrates matters.) From time to time, this stuff must be forked out of the storage pits and disposed of, somehow. Alan spreads a lot of it on his fields. And each year he honours me with two or three trailerloads.

Sheep manure is very hot stuff, I find. Plenty of nitrogen. It is also furnished with an abundance of weed seeds, sheep being fairly indiscriminate eaters (one of the few green things they won't touch is standing nettles, though they'll eat nettles that have been cut). So I have made a practice of letting the manure rot for a year before using it. It does this a couple of hundred yards away from the house, at the far end of my horseshoe pitch. I'd prefer it to be less conspicuous, but that's the only place Alan can reach easily with his tractor and trailer.

In case you've never had occasion to do it, let me tell you that hauling loads of solid, wet sheep manure from pile to garden is no pleasure to humans, however much the result may please members of the vegetable kingdom. Spreading it evenly is difficult, too, although I'm no precisionist; I figure that when you dig it in — which I'm able to do with a tiller in the vegetable garden — it will blend in satisfactorily providing the clay is not too dry or too wet to break up at the same time. In the flowerbeds we simply fork it around as a kind of mulch and hope that it settles in. It usually does.

The problem is that I really don't see much improvement overall in the condition of the soil. It is still recognizably Old Red Sandstone in embryo, just waiting for a few million years of pressure to turn it into first-rate building material. There are places in the vegetable garden where you could chop the earth into fairly plausible bricks; if it were the right colour you could sell it to Royal Doulton to make teapots out of. Even the sheep manure hasn't done the trick, at least not yet.

According to Tom Christopher and Marty Asher, in a funny and pointed (if aggressively titled) new tract *Compost This Book!*, there may still be an answer. In their opinion, salvation lies in the pile. The world is about to be overwhelmed by an avalanche (wave, rising tide — you pick the metaphor) of solid waste. Composting offers a way to get rid of it, thus saving the earth from endless landfills. It also — and this is what I like the sound of — produces a magical substance capable of improving particular small pieces of the earth, such as my garden. If I persist, dutifully composting leaves, grass clippings, hedge trimmings, decayed lettuces, eggshells, potato peelings and other indoor and outdoor miscellanea, and digging in the resulting humus, sooner or later the clay will become black and friable and I will be able to plant my Pink Fir Apple potatoes in April, when I should.

I want to believe this. After all, I have been composting in a fairly shiftless manner for years. When I lived in the Berkshires in Massachusetts, my standard practice involved the use of an old cellar hole just across the road from the house. This measured perhaps 15 feet square and was about 5 feet deep. Every autumn I would fill it up with leaves – mostly maple – and in the summer unsystematically add grass clippings. Occasionally, when I was lucky enough to have some, I would toss in a few shovelfuls of cow manure. In the spring I'd climb into the hole and dig down through the matted leaves until I hit what I supposed was humus. It tended to be black and firm and moist, but broke up readily into sweet-smelling, crumbly stuff like rich earth. Every year I got fifteen or twenty barrowloads, some of which I sieved for use on the flower beds, and the rest – lumpy as it was – tilled straight into the vegetable garden.

Reading Christopher and Asher, I now know that I wasn't doing it right. What I harvested was probably more in the nature of unripe compost than real humus – i.e., it hadn't fully cooked. (While it improved the tilth, it had to go on rotting for a while in the ground and stole, in the process, some of the nitrates found there. This deprived the plants.) I never made any attempt to cover the pile, so rain beat on it and probably leached out most of the nutrients. It never even occurred to me to stir up the pile or turn it over, and in the winter it (like everything else in the neighbourhood) froze solid, which presumably brought the composting process to an abrupt halt. Still, the texture of the resulting soil in my garden could hardly be faulted. Give it a good tilling in April or early May and in August, and you could still thrust your hand in it up to the wrist.

I'm encouraged to see that Asher at least has my own feckless attitude towards the technical side of composting (Christopher is more serious). His original humble pile (nicely termed the Uriah Heap) bears a close resemblance to the one that has gradually been growing like a giant molehill behind a hedge at Towerhill Cottage. His apparently worked, and so has mine, in the sense that something more compost-like comes out than goes in. As *Compost This Book!* points out, 'compost happens' whether you do it right or just do it. So long as you heap up plausible substances in sufficient bulk, they will eventually decay into something useful. It may, of course, take years.

And that's the main thing I've learned from Christopher and Asher – in composting, it's speed that separates the men from the boys. Anybody can create compost (or, as they pronounce it over here, 'compust', with a short 'o') sooner or later, but only those who take some care will get it fast. This means:

1. getting the correct balance of nitrogenous materials (grass clippings, manure, potato peels) to carbon-rich materials (leaves, paper, sawdust) – about 1 to 25 or 30;
2. making the pile big enough – at least 1 cubic yard or so;
3. keeping it moist (not wet);
4. turning it over from time to time to keep it light and aerated.

These seem to be the essentials. From here on things get more complicated: special containers and bins, thermometers to tell you when the pile is 'working', testing gear to measure pH values. I have no real wish to get into that.

I am willing to go a bit farther, however. I have salvaged half a dozen big pieces of corrugated iron which I intend to convert into three compost bins. They will replace my own Uriah-like heap. With these, and years of digging, plus, of course, the Wormery, there is every chance that I can save, if not the earth, my own small piece of it.

The Booby-trapped Carrot

One morning last summer, June Williams peered out of the window of her house in the small Oxfordshire village of Crays Pond to find that someone had stolen the hedge. The whole hedge – 10 feet of well-trimmed, shoulder-high cypress – was gone. 'I couldn't believe what had happened,' she said. 'I had a good laugh about it, but it will cost £400 to replace.' As an afterthought, the thieves also copped a statue of a cherub and a stone watering trough.

Kleptomania is not something I would previously have associated with gardening, sticky fingers normally being considered a consequence of pruning in the wrong season. Mrs Williams, however, is hardly alone these days in suffering from it. According to Scotland Yard, which actually has officers specializing in plant theft, a true crime wave is washing over rural Britain. With gardening the second most expensive hobby in the country – only music buffs spend more on their records, tapes and CDs than the £26 billion a year spent by gardeners on tools, plants and other gear – there are apparently more and more things around to steal. They may or may not be rooted.

There is, of course, nothing particularly new about the theft of expensive garden equipment – mowers, tillers, chainsaws and the like. We have a lot of local criminals of a low-grade sort –

salmon poaching in the Wye still seems to account for a fair number of magistrate-court cases in our area, for example, and nearly every week the *Monmouthshire Beacon and Forest of Dean Gazette* has half a dozen little items about break-ins and thefts. I read these with care, mentally checking just how close they are getting to Towerhill Cottage. The nearest so far is about a quarter of a mile, but we have attentive neighbours just across the lane. There used to be a sign down at the corner saying POLICE, which I'm sure helped, even though there were no police to go with it, and we have recently organized a largely theoretical Neighbourhood Watch Scheme. Still, most people – me included, though reluctantly – tend to keep garages and outbuildings locked, while possession of a large, loud dog and/ or sensor-controlled floodlights is increasingly popular. The latter can be most unsettling when they flash on without warning. I sometimes feel about them the way the Duke of Wellington felt about a ragtag draft of troops sent to him in Spain: 'I don't know what effect these men will have on the enemy, but, by God, they frighten *me*.'

More vulnerable than power equipment – at least you can lock up that sort of thing – are the various bits of what auctioneers like to call 'garden furniture' that form such an important part of many British gardens. Under this heading comes everything from stone fountains to gnomes (though I have to say that there is less call for gnomes by the day), including all kinds of ornamental and functional items in stone, lead or terracotta. As a rule they are supposed to stand in quiet, decorative splendour in the garden itself, but, depending on their weight, most can obviously be lifted. There is a sound and growing market for them too.

According to the International Council on Monuments and Sites, the last five years have seen thefts of garden objects increase from almost nil to nearly half of all art thefts in Britain. Powis Castle in Wales, for example, whose world-famous gardens boast much fine statuary, lost three handsome eighteenth-century figures and a couple of valuable lead urns. At other stately homes, thieves have been known to bridge a ha-ha with planks and drive away the owner's tractor, towing a trailerful of loot. *Country Life*, the *Family Circle* of the fox-hunting classes, went so far recently as to publish a handy guide to alarming, fastening down and otherwise protecting your outdoor valuables. My favourite involves a thumbnail-sized transponder of a type invented to track stolen motorcycles. You embed it in the object, which is then traceable and identifiable even if it turns up in a car-boot in, say, John O'Groats.

Personally, I have not managed to accumulate much in the way of garden furniture. I do have two fragments of old carved stone window tracery and a couple of small stone troughs; it wouldn't take much to spirit them away if some blackguard with a pick-up truck were so inclined. I have no statuary, which may be just as well; in addition to the alarm systems, *Country Life* says you should consider anchoring statues with stainless-steel pins set into solid concrete foundations, which seems like a lot of fuss. I'm not convinced that this would discourage the truly determined anyway. A better solution might be the one recommended by Roy Strong, who buys cheap cement castings of baroque nymphs and Neptunes, and then paints them with milk for a few months. The result, in our climate, is a lovely green-grey patina that makes a £25 fake look like an escapee from Versailles. The statue may still be stolen, but you have the satisfaction of knowing that somebody has gained a bad back to no purpose.

Another real growth area in garden robbery is the plants themselves. Commercial nurseries have a substantial problem: at

Endsleigh Garden Centre, near Plymouth, things got so bad that after £50,000 in theft losses the proprietors had to ban 200 suspected shrub thieves and distribute mug shots to staff. But the field of play is much wider. Thousands of private gardens in Britain are open to visitors either occasionally or every day; there are dozens of major and minor horticultural establishments, from the Royal Botanical Gardens at Kew to the National Digitalis Collection; and countless stately homes, university gardens and municipal parks invite plant lovers to drop in. Most of these have, to some extent, fallen victim to secateurs and trowels.

Stephen Anderton, horticultural officer for English Heritage's northern region, figures that there are two kinds of thief responsible for most of the dirty work, both of them elderly and female. The first is 'the coach-party ladies who seem to think that since they have paid, they can take home samples'. The other consists of more knowledgeable gardeners intent on picking up rarities for themselves or to order. 'You find the most unlikely people doing it,' Anderton says. At Belsay Hall, in Northumberland, he caught three women from a Mothers' Union outing filling up their handbags with cuttings. The oldest, eighty, was the mother of one of the two sixty-year-olds. They said it was all her idea.

Like a cat burglar checking out the diamonds on display in a Monte Carlo casino, plant thieves do their homework. If television's *Gardeners' World* demonstrates on a Friday night how to take cuttings from a particular species, you can be pretty sure to find that species thoroughly snipped by Saturday evening. The National Trust, which supervises many of the most important gardens in Britain, has reportedly lost so much valuable material that it now waits to label some plants until they are fully grown, in hopes that ignorance will cause thieves to hesitate about taking cuttings. Or, for that matter, lifting the plants bodily.

According to Scotland Yard, certain plant-nappers use a garden visit as a casing expedition, then come back at night with a spade and a truck. Police suggestions for dealing with this sort of thing include making paths out of gravel for a tell-tale crunch, and planting unfriendly hedges. They have prepared a list of ten 'thorny, prickly, and hostile' varieties, including berberis, rugosa roses and holly.

Personally, we have yet to lose a plant to marauders other than slugs, rabbits and aphids, but then we live pretty deep in the backwoods. I worry more about the pile of old flagstones waiting to be laid than about an especially shapely hebe or the new Blenheim Orange apple tree or the ceanothus with the deep-blue blossoms. An hour or so east of us in the Cotswolds, where there is a lot more money, many more second-home owners and an abundance of splendid gardens, people are a great deal less relaxed, judging from newspaper reports. Even vegetable gardens have become fair game. In Oxford itself hundreds of thefts have been reported from allotments, where city dwellers grow cabbages, turnips and the occasional prizewinning pumpkin. One elderly pensioner had his entire crop of potatoes stolen by thieves who then replanted the tops. 'The old boy had poor eyesight and went on watering his plants for days,' said the investigating policeman. 'He was heartbroken when he found out what had happened.'

In a furious article in the *Independent* newspaper last summer, Duff Hart-Davis allowed as how the time had come for striking back. 'I myself favour trip-wires fitted to simple alarm guns that fire blank twelve-bore cartridges and make bangs loud enough to awaken the dead.' But more radical measures should be considered – 'explosive parsnips or thunderflash carrots, which would detonate when touched'. I found one of his ideas especially appropriate: fix a canister of anaesthetizing gas to go off when a burglar arrives. Then, like the Flopsy Bunnies sleeping off that soporific lettuce in Mr MacGregor's vegetable patch, he'd still be there in the morning.

Such aggressiveness can have its own drawbacks. Eighty-two-year-old Ted Newbery was recently ordered to pay £4,000 compensation to a burglar he blasted with a shotgun when he caught the man trying to break into his garden shed. Admittedly, Newbery had previously turned the shed into a virtual fort, and was lying in wait with the gun trained through a hole in the door.

On reflection, I suppose we should not be too surprised at the thought of malfeasance in the garden. I see that the editor of an American gardening magazine was recently quoted as saying that 'the garden has everything: sex, drama, life and death,' so what's a little crime? Besides, the British take gardens more seriously than other people do. When Sarah Potter, a resident of Cullompton in Devon, noticed that many of the plants in her garden were mysteriously dying, even after replanting, she set up a camcorder in her living-room window and taped her neighbours pouring what was later found to be sodium chlorate from a teacup over the fence into the Potter flowers. In court the Daveys' defence was that *their* garden had been looking peaked too, and they strongly suspected Mrs Potter of secret herbicide. Lacking a camcorder, the Daveys lost. On the whole, simple theft might have been easier.

It may at this point be worth remembering the old Turkish method of dealing with such matters. The head gardener at the sultan's Topkapi palace by tradition always had a second job. It was chief executioner.

GARDENERS AND OTHER OBSESSIVES

Darwin and the Earthworms

Charlie Wilcox, my neighbour in the Berkshires in Massachusetts, used to talk about how New England gardens raised stones. It didn't seem to matter how many you levered out; the next year there were always more. The tiller would leap into the air like a wild thing, and you'd know that it was time to get out the pry bar, an old cold-forged Model T axle. After a certain amount of digging and heaving on the bar, another boulder would emerge. Granted that bedrock wasn't very far down (locals called it 'ledge'), it never ceased to amaze me how each spring there was a new crop of stones, large and small, among the vegetables.

Oddly enough, according to Charles Darwin, the stones should have been sinking. This comes to mind because I've been working lately (as an editor only, mind you) on a new biography of the great man. Like most people, I never knew much about Darwin, except that he took a trip aboard a ship called the *Beagle* and discovered evolution; in my mind he was one of those larger-than-life Victorian figures with a huge beard and even bigger ideas, a man with no time for the sort of interesting but pointless things you and I think about.

It pleases me to know now that I was wrong. When Darwin's uncle (and future father-in-law) described him as 'a man of enlarged curiosity', he was barely stating the case. Because Darwin, I learn, was wonderfully, irrepressibly, comprehensively curious. He cared about, studied, puzzled over and, what's more, wrote about all manner of things, from beetles to volcanoes, kidney beans to inherited instincts. If he was prepared to theorize about the development of species, he was also ready to investigate why his holly trees had no berries in the winter of 1877, how a Venus-flytrap works or whether small moths suck flowers (and, if so, what flowers).

For example, in 1861 we find him reporting to the *Gardener's Chronicle and Agricultural Gazette* his success in fertilizing *Vinca major* 'with a fine bristle to represent the proboscis of a moth'; he intended to sow the resulting seeds, 'for a plant which seeds so rarely might be expected to give way to some freak on so unusual and happy an occasion'. (I wish I knew what happened.) Another communication to the *Gardener's Chronicle* inquired whether any readers had experience with wire rope. 'I suffer from the serious misfortune,' he said, 'of a well 325 feet deep' with a commensurately heavy chain. (The wire rope worked fine. His next question concerned the bucket: 'Must I stick to my old oaken friend?')

Then there was The Appearance of a Plant in a Singular Place. It seems that an *Epipactis latifolia* (a wild orchid) inexplicably emerged one day in the middle of a gravel walk at Down House, Darwin's home in Kent. The walk had been made twenty years before, and that particular variety of orchid was locally rare. The discovery naturally merited a letter to the *Gardener's Chronicle*. The Singular Plant itself – carefully preserved from trampling feet – came in handy half a dozen years later for study during a survey of the ways different orchids are fertilized.

You might get the impression from this sort of thing that

Darwin was frivolous, but he surely wasn't. At the same time as he was noting such trivia, he was not only working out his epochal ideas on natural selection but also seriously investigating a wide variety of related (and wildly unrelated) phenomena. In his *Collected Papers* may be found long, learned essays on geology, biochemistry, botany, ornithology and more. He was clearly fascinated by plants, especially flowers, and many of his experiments concerned the ways they fertilized themselves or attracted insects to do the job. Among his nearly two dozen books are volumes on insectivorous plants and on the power of movement in plants. At the other extreme, he once conducted a correspondence in print on the mystery of the beheaded primroses in his garden. The culprits turned out to be bullfinches in search of nectar.

Possibly the best example of Darwin's 'enlarged curiosity' was his interest in – almost obsession with – earthworms. It apparently began not long after the conclusion of his four-year voyage on the *Beagle*, when he was visiting Maer, the Wedgwood country estate in Staffordshire. As he reported in a short paper delivered to the Geological Society of London, Uncle Josiah had called to his attention a possible explanation for the formation of what was then called 'mould' – the dark, fertile topsoil blessed by every farmer and gardener. Examining several fields that had been spread with lime a few years before, and others spread with burned marl and cinders, Wedgwood noticed that the lime, marl and cinders had mysteriously sunk beneath the surface. They hadn't dispersed but had simply *sunk*, still in a perceptible, intact layer. In another field, ploughed, harrowed and fertilized with burned lime and cinders some fifteen years earlier, the marl–cinder layer was now covered with no less than 4 inches of mould – 'fine particles of earth mixed with decayed vegetable matter'.

Wedgwood's notion, which Darwin supported, was at first blush an improbable one. Others might lay the phenomenon of sinking cinders to gravity or rain or some unknown agency, but Wedgwood and Darwin believed 'the whole operation is due to the digestive process of the common earthworm'. Munching his way through the earth and unassimilated vegetable debris, expelling the finely mixed and enriched fragments in the form of casts *on the surface*, the worm was little by little burying anything left on the ground and, incidentally, creating exactly what most plants can't do without.

Darwin read his paper in 1837. Now forty years go by. We find him an august – if controversial – figure, massively white-bearded, living out his days at Down House. He has considered pedunculated cirripedes, he has discoursed upon the variations of animals and plants under domestication, he has raised a fine family of five boys and two girls and, so far as most people are concerned, he has invented evolution. But he hasn't forgotten earthworms. Far from it.

In June 1877 his wife, Emma, writes to their son George: 'F[ather] was made very happy by finding two old stones at the bottom of the field, and he has now got a man digging for the worms . . .' They plan a trip to Stonehenge: 'I'm afraid it will half-kill F. . . . but he is bent on going, chiefly for the worms.' Back home again: 'They did not find much good about the worms, who seem to be very idle out there.' In the summer of 1880: 'F. has no proof sheets and has taken to training earthworms but does not make much progress as they can neither see nor hear. They are, however, amusing and spend hours in seizing hold of the edge of a cabbage leaf and trying in vain to pull it into their holes.'

What has happened is that in all those forty years, Charles Darwin has never stopped brooding about earthworms and 'vegetable mould'. He has put down marker layers on fields to see what would happen (almost the first thing he did upon settling at Down House in 1842 was to spread chunks of chalk in a meadow), taking soundings every decade or two; he has canvassed the literature for facts on world worm distribution; he has travelled all over southern England examining ruined Roman villas and prehistoric monuments, in order to measure subsidence caused by worm activity. Reading the plump little book he produced to describe his experiments and report his startled findings, we can only admire – and delight in, if we possess even a fraction of his 'enlarged curiosity' – the ingenuity and enterprise with which this septuagenarian, dogged by ill health, burrowed into the mysteries of the earthworm universe.

With the assistance of his sons Francis and Bernard (the former would become a distinguished botanist, the latter an equally – or more – distinguished writer on golf!), Darwin tested the earthworm's capacity for sight (virtually nil) and hearing (likewise, although there seemed to be some reaction to C in the treble clef when he played the note on a piano; both a whistle and a bassoon went unappreciated). 'Feeble' was his judgement of a worm's sense of smell. And as for 'Mental Qualities' – well, 'there is little to be said'. A *Lumbricus terrestris* did seem to have some dim idea of which corner to grab when it came to pulling a dead leaf into its burrow, but not always.

But if worms were rather lacking in sensitivity, other experiments made plain that they were wonderfully competent in the way that mattered – specifically, in creating mould. Magisterially, Darwin spells it out: 'A single worm produces perhaps 20 ounces of castings a year . . . Hensen estimates that garden soil contains 53,767 worms per acre . . . weighed castings collected from a grassed terrace demonstrate a rate of 7.56 tons of dry earth a year per acre passed by earthworms . . . near Nice 14.58

tons . . . Leith Hill Common 16.1 tons . . . a poor chalk pasture
18.15 tons . . .' The statistics tumble forth, impressively, irrefut-
ably. No wonder the chalk and cinders sank, no wonder the great
toppled megaliths of Stonehenge lie half buried in the ground,
no wonder 'farmers in England are well aware that objects of all
kinds, left on the surface of pasture-land, after a time disappear,
or, as they say, work themselves downwards'. And, what is more
important to us, no wonder the earth is rich and loamy, and
welcoming to growing things. 'Worms,' Darwin concludes with
satisfaction, 'have played a more important part in the history of
the world than most persons would at first suppose.'

Modern soil scientists may take a more complicated view; no
doubt there is a lot more than wriggling going on in humus.
After all, nobody was in a position to pay much attention to
bacteria and microscopic fungi in 1881, and it's now known that
they play a considerably larger role in breaking down organic
matter and creating soil fertility than does the gizzard of a
Lumbricus.

As for the sinking stones, the situation is more complicated,
too. A retired dentist named Lyne studied his own array of
worm pots and concluded that the rootlets of turf, by attacking
and absorbing worm casts, were at least partly responsible for
burying surface objects. And when Sir Arthur Keith went back
in 1941 to see where Darwin's chalk had got to in 100 years, he
found that moles had so confused the issue that some pieces –
which had been under 7 inches of mould in 1871 – were actually
on the surface again! (This could explain Charlie Wilcox's growing stones, I suppose, if you substitute woodchucks for moles,
but I suspect that frost has a lot more to do with it. Frost is a
great stone-shifter, generally in an upward direction, and if
Darwin ignored it, remember that it gets far colder in New
England than it does in Kent.)

Nevertheless, Darwin's basic thesis – that earthworms are prime movers in the creation of a pleasant growing medium, finely divided and stone-free – seems indisputable. Everyone with a gardenful should be grateful.

It is nice to note that his worm book, Darwin's last, brought forth under the uncompromising title *The Formation of Mould through the Action of Worms, with Observations on Their Habits*, outsold anything else he published during his lifetime, even *On the Origin of Species*. It was, in fact, a bestseller, going to more than 8,000 copies in fewer than three years. The author himself was confounded. 'It has been a complete surprise to me,' he said, 'how many persons have cared for the subject.'

Loudon

In the spring of the year, about the time of the early daffodils or the late *Prunus subbirtella*, garden-book announcements begin to blossom in the publishing trade press. The quantity and variety is truly marvellous. Here are shiny stacks of blockbusters, books of instruction and books of inspiration, books filled with pictures in glorious colour, books offering the last word (until next year) on everything from epiphytes to truffles, dogwoods to harebells, sequoias to bonsai. Where do all these ideas come from? Can the fertility of a publisher's loam hope to match the fertility of his imagination? In the midst of such thoughts I am reminded again of the greatest garden writer of them all, at least in terms of sheer volume: John Claudius Loudon.

I first ran across Loudon a couple of years ago when I was trawling the stacks of the London Library in search of information on carpet bedding, that misguided Victorian attempt to turn normal gardens into glaringly colourful, two-dimensional pancakes (see pp. 164–71). The London Library is rich in old volumes, and I was struck by the fact that in the Gardening section (a subdivision of Science, in case you want to know) a surprising number of them seemed to have been written by one J. C. Loudon: *Self-Instruction for Young Gardeners*; *The Suburban Horticulturist*; *The Encyclopaedia of Gardening*; *The Cottager's Manual* of Husbandry; *Architecture, Domestic Economy, and Gardening*; *The Suburban Gardener and Villa Companion*; and too many more to contemplate. They weren't negligible little books, either, but 'damned, square, fat, thick books' (as the Duke of Gloucester complained to Edward Gibbon upon being presented with a volume of *The Decline and Fall of the Roman Empire*), printed in very small type in close-packed columns. The very sight of all those words induced admiration and, I have to admit, vertigo.

So who was John Claudius Loudon? He was a Scotsman, born not far from Edinburgh in 1783. His father was a farmer, by all reports a good one, but young John aspired to more. When he was eleven he became a part-time draughtsman and general assistant to a local nurseryman, landscape gardener and hothouse expert. He also began teaching himself – at a furious pace Latin, French, Greek, Hebrew, German, and Italian, to say nothing of mathematics and history. Sluicing down continual cups of strong green tea in order to stay awake, he frequently studied all night. At twenty, after a short spell at Edinburgh University, he went off to London armed with letters of introduction to such luminaries as the explorer and botanist Sir Joseph Banks and the philosopher Jeremy Bentham. Soon he was practising as a landscape designer, working in the tradition of Humphry Repton on country estates the length and breadth of Britain.

Loudon had not been in England for a year before he was scribbling out plans for refurbishing London's public squares ('to the utmost picturesque advantage') and having them published in the *Literary Journal*. Books began flowing from his pen, one or two a year, on a variety of subjects. He could always find time to write, even if it meant dispatching parcels of copy from inns in Wales or Scotland. In the meantime he kept right on projecting vistas and planting copses, dredging lakes and laying out ornamental beds, the larger the scale the better. And he painted, too, exhibiting landscapes – no better than competent, it must be said – at the Royal Academy.

In 1807 a hitch occurred in Loudon's headlong career, one that would have stopped a lesser man. Travelling back from Wales on the outside of a crowded coach, he caught cold in a rainstorm; the cold turned to rheumatic fever, leaving him with a permanently stiffened knee and a crippled right arm. Nothing daunted, he leased a farm in Middlesex, invited his father down from Scotland to help him, and by the time he was thirty had accumulated a healthy fortune of £15,000 from his combined labours as farmer, land agent and landscape gardener. Plus, of course, writing. With books ranging from *Designs for Farms* to *A Treatise on Wheat*, he scarcely broke stride.

Yet luck was not with Loudon. First, while he was off on an extended foreign tour visiting gardens and hobnobbing with savants all across northern Europe (he got as far as Moscow), his banker managed to lose all his money in inept speculations. Then an over-enthusiastic masseur at Mohamed's Vapour Baths in Brighton, while trying to limber up Loudon's crippled right arm with 'shampoo and stretching', broke it near the shoulder. It never healed properly. He could still use it to write, but barely, and when he broke it again it had to be amputated. Meanwhile the left arm, afflicted with acute rheumatism, was going out of commission as well. Poor Loudon, stuffed full of words and itching to get them on paper, found himself reduced to the use of two fingers on his left hand. Perhaps understandably, he took up opium.

He could still dictate, and did, copiously. In 1822 came the first edition of his mammoth *Encyclopaedia of Gardening*: 1,200 pages, some 1.3 million words, more than 1,000 woodcut illustrations ranging from the Hanging Gardens of Babylon to a brussels sprout. Divided into four sections, it dealt in turn with the history of gardening (pretty much from Eden on), gardening considered as a science, the art and practice of gardening and a statistical survey of British gardening. The general effect was – and is – dazzling, although the tone does tend towards what one critic called 'hectoring instruction'. A German translation began appearing in serial form. Loudon was suddenly famous.

In a memoir of her husband written after his death, his wife remarked that 'Mr Loudon was not a man of many words.' The fact is, he had words to spare. Books were not enough for this fountain of prose. In 1826 he produced the first issue of the *Gardener's Magazine (and Register of Rural and Domestic Improvements)*, a tightly packed little octavo quarterly publication bearing on its title page a vividly symbolic device of surveying instruments, plough, rake, watering can, spade, spool of string for making straight rows and other paraphernalia. Loudon, as 'Director', edited pieces from numerous contributors and wrote all the miscellaneous matter himself – editorials, comments on readers' letters, reports of new techniques and machinery. Leafing through the pages, one hears his voice clearly enough, brisk and forthright and occasionally exasperated. Replying, for example, to a nurseryman in Albany, New York, who had sent him a bundle of grafts and wanted some in return, the overworked editor sputtered: 'To be able to live at all in this country, is too engrossing a business, to allow of much else occupying the time than the means by which we get our daily bread.' (No grafts for Albany, apparently.) Printed without comments, however, were articles on such useful subjects as weeding techniques, forcing mushrooms and 'the best modes of washing Water Cresses and other Salads, so as to free them from the larvae of insects and worms'.

The *Gardener's Magazine* was soon appearing monthly and turning a profit of £750 a year. Gathering his financial resources, Loudon designed himself a handsome little villa in Bayswater, then on the outskirts of London, just north of Kensington Gardens. The garden, stocked with what eventually amounted to 2,000 species of plants, served as a sort of testing ground for his horticultural experiments.

His frantic labours had appeared to doom him to a bachelor existence, but in 1830 he met a much younger woman named Jane Wells Webb. This time luck was with him because she was an aspiring writer. She was also attractive, calm and from a respectable, if financially embarrassed, Yorkshire family. Her most notable publication until then had been a novel set in the twenty-first century called *The Mummy*, and she confessed to knowing nothing whatever about gardening. Marrying her forthwith (and, with his usual single-mindedness, continuing to dictate even while his valet was dressing him for the wedding), he quickly made her a key part of the Porchester Terrace writing factory. Together the Loudons actually increased the flow of printed words and incidentally produced a daughter named Agnes.

It should be noted that Loudon and his wife were principled bookwrights. They were not in it simply for the money. In her study of Loudon, Melanie Louise Simo points out how up to the time of the *Encylopaedia*, he produced mainly expensive and elegant tomes for the gentry. From then on, he saw his main audience as 'self-educated, self-improving young gardeners, craftsmen and middle-class householders'. And heaven knows there were plenty of them around. From his own experience, as well as the influence of such reform-minded acquaintances as Bentham and Robert Owen, he was dedicated to the idea that the world could be made a better place to live in, even if you had to start with clear instructions for making oiled paper caps to protect your dahlias.

The *Gardener's Magazine* ran for nearly twenty years. During this period Loudon – with Jane's help – also edited several other periodicals, on gardening, natural history and architecture. At one hectic point in 1836, the team was putting out *five* substantial monthly publications simultaneously. The atmosphere in Porchester Terrace must have been electric. But Loudon was, as one reviewer commented, 'indefatigable'. Jane herself marvelled in her memoir: 'Deducting the time he has been poorly, he has, during three-quarters of his literary career, dictated about five-and-a-half printed octavo pages of matter every day on average.' (This works out to nearly 6,000 words. At that rate he might have produced a longish novel every three weeks.) Sometimes he dictated to two copyists at the same time.

In the early 1830s Loudon started work on a *magnum opus*. The resoundingly titled *Arboretum et Fruticetum Britannicum* was to be a complete descriptive and anecdotal catalogue of British trees, a celebration of the plants he was convinced had not received proper attention from landscape designers and gardeners. He sent out 3,000 questionnaires to estate owners all over the country, inquiring about interesting trees on their properties. Because of Loudon's fame and reputation, the response was overwhelming. Travelling and scholarly research filled out the details, and in 1834 the first lavish volume emerged from the press. By 1837 the work – now twice the four volumes originally planned – was complete.

Against all advice, Loudon had insisted on funding the project himself, mortgaging the income from his other works to do so. The result was a burden of debt as crippling as his physical infirmities. A worldwide depression affected the book trade, and sales failed to cover his huge £10,000 investment. Sick as he was, he had to return to landscape design to make a living.

The end was not long in coming. Loudon laid out a few country seats. He designed and planted the Derby Arboretum. He produced plans for several cemeteries and wrote a book (the last he completed) *On the Laying Out, Planting, and Management of Cemeteries and the Improvement of Churchyards*. (He didn't really approve of conventional cemeteries, suggesting that crema-tion made more sense; the ashes could then 'be preserved in urns, or applied to the roots of a favourite plant'.) In 1843, diagnosed as having a fatal lung disease, he wrote in some desperation to a number of wealthy men urging them to buy copies of the *Arboretum*. ('If this work does not repay the author for his immense labour,' *Gentleman's Magazine* had declared, 'the public deserves to be gibbeted on the trees which they have not had the sense or the taste to value.') Some responded, enough to save him from bankruptcy. But two weeks later, while dictating *Self-Instruction for Young Gardeners*, he collapsed and died in Jane's arms. In America, A. J. Downing wrote that 'his Her-culean labors have at last destroyed him', and mourned him as 'one who has done more than any other person that ever lived to popularize, and render universal, a taste for gardening and domestic architecture'. Jane inherited a debt of £2,400.

Heroically, she picked up the pieces. Friends helped reduce the debt. She doggedly revised and reissued her husband's works, and wrote more of her own, including such charm-ing and influential books as *Gardening for Ladies* and *The Lady's Country Companion, or How to Enjoy a Country Life Ration-ally*. And into her declining years, she lived on at Porchester Terrace.

The house still stands, now cramped in among many others on a fairly posh (and frightfully expensive) street in Bayswater, with a garden that is no more than rudimentary. Of all those hundreds of books, magazines, pamphlets and what-have-you – all those words – almost nothing remains in print.

Edward Augustus Bowles

As gardeners we are, I suppose, all amateurs now. The categories have become pretty blurry, and even here in Britain there aren't many horny-handed old professionals left. Such distinctions used to be firmer, as the case of Edward Augustus Bowles amply testifies. Bowles (1865–1956) is often described as the greatest *amateur* gardener of his day. Personally, I'm inclined to call anybody who devoted all of his waking hours through most of a long life to growing plants, collecting plants, studying plants, classifying plants, writing about plants, exchanging plants and admiring plants a professional of the first water. But Bowles – and this is the real point – didn't do it for money. He didn't have to, being the heir to a comfortable fortune, including a Georgian mansion with extensive grounds on the northern edge of London. His hired garderners may have been professionals, but – make no mistake about it – Gus Bowles was an amateur.

We should all be such amateurs. Beginning about 1893, and continuing for sixty years, Bowles developed a garden at Myddelton House that for beauty and interest rivalled much greater and more famous spreads. He made particular collections of certain species – irises, for example, and crocuses – disentangling their botanical heritages at the same time as he was growing them to perfection. On dozens of springtime expeditions to the Dolomites, to Greece and elsewhere (his hay fever drove him out of England each June), he searched out rare alpines and brought them back – along with the odd unusual frog or lizard. He built a rock garden, he built an alpine meadow, he built a pond with stone terraces, he built pergolas and walls and an avenue of standard roses. And, for which he most deserves our gratitude, he wrote three wonderful books.

My Garden in Spring, *My Garden in Summer* and *My Garden in Autumn and Winter* all came out just as the guns of August 1914 were thundering across Europe and bringing an era to a close. Things would never be the same in the great gardens of England. No longer were teams of workmen ready to answer the whims of gentleman amateurs by digging lakes or planting groves for a few pence a day. But Bowles had never been that sort of 'amateur' anyway.

On the contrary, he was a strictly hands-on man and, moreover, a gardener with a close and intense interest in his plants. There is something very modern here, and it helps to explain why his books still have the power to charm. They are about his garden – but they are also about Edward Augustus Bowles.

His approach could not be more forthright. Without writing down to readers, or poleaxing us with too much technical information, he systematically moves through the garden, describing plants, telling us where he got them, talking about varieties, commenting on where they grow best (or fail) and his experiences in propagating them. Unhesitatingly, he will wander off the immediate subject into some engaging, if loosely related, point (impatiently explaining that there *isn't* any difference between narcissi and daffodils); call our attention to something that annoys or pleases him ('I confess to adoring Scarlet Pelargoniums'); give a bit of history or advice ('patience seems to be the only manure [*Iris unguicularis*] need'). His delight in his garden and its inhabitants is palpable, and so is his firm disdain for certain species – zinnias, clarkias, gaillardias, cactus, dahlias, 'spotty, marbled double balsams I should like to smash up with a coal-hammer' – which will never find a place there.

It is clear that at heart Bowles was a plantsman, not a garden designer or builder, and I don't mean that negatively. He viewed plants almost as individuals, and talked about them that way. 'I feel sorry for plants,' he wrote, 'that are obliged to make a struggle for life in uncongenial situations because their owner wishes all things of those shades of pink, or blue, or orange to fit in next to the grey or crimson planting . . .' Thus he spent years working out the precise soil, drainage and aspect conditions needed for his Tyrolean primulas and was perfectly willing to put a 'choice young Eucalyptus in a pot' in the middle of the alpine bed if it was comfortable there. 'So long as plants flourish I cannot bring myself to destroy their happiness.'

If this sounds like a recipe for a hopeless jumble, any visitor to Myddelton can see that it didn't work out that way. Bowles seems to have had a natural feeling for organization along with his horticultural sensibility. In *My Garden in Autumn and Winter*, for instance, he puzzled over how to interplant autumn crocuses: 'Certainly the effect of the flowers rising through some Acaena or Saxifrage is good, but unless the Crocuses are scattered rather thinly there is a risk of the carpet being bothered and worried into a nervous breakdown or anaemic debility from having to struggle with a mass of long crocus leaves lying on it . . . Now I am trying *C. speciosus* in a carpet of ivy . . .'

Of course, sometimes Bowles's organizational tactics could be eccentric. One of his more famous innovations – I almost wrote institutions – was the Lunatic Asylum. This was a section in the garden set aside for a 'home for demented plants' – plants that in some way or other grew in a perverse or improbable manner.

The first of these – and 'perhaps the maddest of all, even now' – was a contorted hazel, *Corylus avellana*, 'a collection of various curves and spirals, a tangle of crooks and corkscrews from root to tip'. (It was then a rarity. Bowles got his from Canon Ellacombe, another prominent gardener-writer, who in turn is supposed to have received a cutting from its original discoverer, one Lord Ducie, who found it growing in a hedge near Bristol. Contorted hazel is now readily available in nurseries.) Other inmates included a common elder that insisted on growing upright, 'as straight and stiff as a grenadier', a dwarf ash, several odd plaintains and a miniature guelder rose that, 'suffering from melancholy madness', never flowered.

His alpine meadow had another kind of logic behind it, though it too focused upon the plants themselves and their individual wishes. In this case, his aim was a natural ensemble. At first it was just a dream. In 1914, writing in *My Garden in Summer*, he devoted a chapter to grasses, which (in spite of his hay fever) fascinated him. The very 'beau ideal of a large flower bed', he declared, was a grassy meadow spangled with plants such as *Salvia pratensis*, alpine anemones, primulas and crocuses. 'I should be proud as a dog with two tails,' he wrote, 'if someone with greater space and leisure, and more gardeners and bawbees than I possess, should be fired by this chapter to bring the idea to perfection.' Four years later the coins (and presumably the gardeners) were to hand: his father died and left him the house and the gardens, and the first thing he did was convert a sloping field below the rock garden to the ideal flower bed. Beginning in the spring with white spring snowflakes (*Leucojum* species), then little early daffodils, crocuses, fritillaries, camassias and, finally, blue crane's-bill geraniums as high summer approached, it was a mountain meadow straight out of the Italian Alps.

Like every gardener, Bowles complained about his soil (far

too light and gravelly) and the climate ('I cannot believe that there is a drier garden to be found in England'). In fact, of course, a river ran through it. The so-called New River was an aqueduct, built by an ancestor in the late seventeenth century as a foresighted business venture. It brought much needed clean water from springs in Hertfordshire down to the city and was, among other things, the foundation of the Bowles family fortune. As a garden feature, however, it was less useful. The riverbed had been carefully caulked and battered with clay to prevent leakage, and in any case the water was 'so hard that one feels it would be scarcely a miracle to walk on it'. It allegedly killed rhododendrons watered with it during a drought.

We can be sure that Bowles was circumspect about his use of New River water. More than one observer commented upon his talent for judging exactly what a plant needed to thrive, and it is plain that he possessed an unusual sympathy for his charges. He talks about them like children – this one is 'miffy' (as in 'difficult and miffy'), that one 'unreliable and pernickety'. His biographer Mea Allan notes how his valet despaired of his tendency to begin digging and weeding at the most inappropriate moments, generally wearing his best clothes; pictures show him kneeling in a border dressed in coat and tie and highly polished shoes. For a short while he carried a cake of soap with him in a box so that he could claw his fingernails full of it ('as a cat claws a tree or the leg of one's best Chippendale chairs') and keep them from getting dirty. (Needless to say, this 'most refined and elegant' enterprise didn't last.)

Bowles's immediate, almost human, involvement with the plants in his garden, and the eagerness, enthusiasm and curiosity that shine in his writing, go some way towards explaining what kind of man he was. A child of Victorian England, educated for the Church but forced to give up any thought of a career when one of his brothers, and then his sister, died of tuberculosis and left him to live with his ageing parents, Bowles never married. His friendships, largely within the gardening community, were extensive, and nearer home he was mentor, sponsor and benefactor of literally dozens of neighbourhood boys. They clustered, as his biographer says, around him like bees, helping in the garden, listening to him talk. He apparently talked wonderfully to children and for many years wrote (as 'Uncle G') nature notes for a children's magazine.

But Bowles was much more than a popularizer. In addition to his three classic garden guides, he also produced definitive works on daffodils and crocuses and published numerous scholarly papers. He developed hybrids and did a fair amount of serious plant hunting. Dozens of plants bear his name, either because he found them – *Primula bowlesii* ('a mawkish magenta' primrose), for example, and *Vinca minor* 'Bowles's Variety' (more accurately known as 'La Grave', which became extremely popular in both England and America after he brought home a few runners from an alpine churchyard) – or because he first raised or refined them: *Buxus sempervirens* 'Bowles's Blue', two hebes ('Bowles's Hybrid' and 'E. A. Bowles'), a hellebore called 'Bowles Yellow', and many more. Particularly notable, mainly for its name, is the little pansy *Viola nigra* 'E. A. Bowles', otherwise known uneuphoniously as 'Bowles Black'.

Bowles was also an artist, and, with accuracy and a delicate touch, drew and painted watercolours. (In 1901 he grew no fewer than 135 species of crocuses and colchicums, and as each opened he painted an exact portrait of it.) For fifty years he was a mainstay of the Royal Horticultural Society and a familiar figure among judges at the Chelsea Flower Show and elsewhere. And his garden – fussed over, added to, tended with abiding love and care even when German bombs were falling on it during World

War II – preserved and even enhanced his fame as one of the most discriminating plantsmen of his day.

Edward Augustus Bowles died in 1956, at the exceedingly ripe age of ninety, no doubt sustained by dabbling in compost all those years. He willed his garden, hopefully, to the Department of Pharmacognosy of the University of London's School of Pharmacy, which established a subsidiary garden for medically significant plants and valiantly undertook to maintain the rest. In 1984 the Lee Valley Regional Park Authority assumed control, using the house as its headquarters and proposing to restore the garden 'in the style of Bowles'. By then it was sadly overgrown. Many valuable plants had disappeared in a maze of nettles and cow-parsley.

I paid a call at Myddelton House last summer and was pleased to see that Bowles's garden still had a reasonably firm claim on posterity. The gardeners – no doubt professionals now – had laboured heroically to bring it back to life. Rain fell steadily upon the shaved lawns as I squished across them (*this* was the driest garden in England?) – they were smooth and handsome in spite of regrettable patches of clover; the avenue of standard roses was fluffy with bloom. In the Lunatic Asylum I found a contorted hazel (plainly not the original) huddling under a huge sycamore and one of Bowles's ancient yews. No doubt there were other mad things more obvious to a trained eye than to mine. Long, wide, spiky iris beds, empty now of bloom, bordered the curving lawn where the New River, rerouted in 1962, used to flow. I tried to find the alpine meadow and the rock garden, but, except for a few blue geraniums and some stumps of Kentish ragstone overgrown with weeds, both have vanished. Hardly surprising, and certainly no cause for complaint, since, as Bowles himself pointed out, you needed plenty of bawbees for that sort of gardening.

I must say I raised an eyebrow at the large bed of pink begonias beside the drive. With characteristic firmness, Bowles had once expressed himself on the subject of begonias: 'I do not like their fat, meaty blossoms and floppy habits, and cannot be bothered with them.' Fortunately for us, he could 'be bothered' with very much else – and was.

Robinson v. *Blomfield*

If there was one thing William Robinson hated – and he was a good hater – it was formality in the garden. He spoke for Nature. As a writer (promoter, explicator, proselytizer) he had made his name opposing the Victorian style, with its painfully artificial carpet bedding and stiff, show-off design; its badly grouped – and often badly grown – shrubs; its uninspired use of a few stereotypical species planted with no thought to seasonal effect. What Robinson liked was the richness and unpredictability of creepers and ramblers, of blossoming hedges, of borders full of flowers and bulbs chosen for their shapes and colours, of roses (never standards) underplanted with a variety of smaller flowers, of shrub beds spacious and airy enough to permit natural development, of cottage gardens billowing with perennials. What he didn't like – apart from bedding, of course – were such things as palm trees ('tropical weeds'), *parterre* and knot gardens, grandiose French landscaping *à la* le Nôtre, vast terraces with bare stonework gleaming unsoftened by climbers or foliage, pretension in general. Formality made William Robinson's beard curl.

By 1892 he had every reason to think that most of his battles had been won. His books – *The Wild Garden* (1870), *Hardy Flowers* (1871), *The English Flower Garden* (1883), and half a dozen more – and his magazines – the *Garden*, *Gardening Illustrated*, *Farm and Home*, and others – had exerted an overwhelming influence on the gardening scene. Bedding was in disgrace, and, in Gertrude Jekyll's view, Robinson killed it off singlehandedly: 'A strong champion arose and fought strenuously to stay the devastating tide, and to restore the healthy liking for the good old garden flowers ... bedding is now dead.' Arguably (though some credit Jekyll), he was the man responsible for the new fashion, one that is still with us: the herbaceous border. He had, moreover, become rich through his efforts. Now, at fifty-four, a self-made man, he was developing his own magnificent garden at Gravetye Manor in Sussex.

It has to be said that Robinson was thin-skinned, and success had made him no less so. Stories of his bad temper went way back. Famously, he was supposed to have walked out in anger one cold winter night from his job as an apprentice gardener on an Irish estate, but not before extinguishing the fires that kept the greenhouses warm; thousands of tender plants froze. His later quarrels ran through the gardening community, and beyond; even Canon Henry Ellacombe, the amiable clergyman who – together with Jekyll and other leading gardeners – had contributed to *The English Flower Garden*, found him impossible to get on with. 'As to Robinson,' Ellacombe wrote, 'I give up trying to get his twist right.' Tenaciously and infuriatingly, Robinson fought for years with Sir Joseph Hooker over Kew's policy of labelling plants with Latin names. In a private letter the architect Sir Edwin Lutyens, who regarded Robinson as 'a foozle headed old bore', commented that 'his conversation [is] wayward and [he] contradicts himself every two minutes.'

There *was* something woolly about Robinson's theoretical positions, though contradictory is probably too strong a term to describe him. He was vastly knowledgeable about plants and horticulture in general. He had wide experience in garden design, and a good eye for natural beauty. But his temper had taken him to the end of more than one limb, and the publication of a little book in a buff binding called *The Formal Garden in England* was to take him to another.

The author of *The Formal Garden* was a young architect named Reginald Blomfield. Much influenced by the Arts and Crafts movement, whose mentors were William Morris and the architect Richard Norman Shaw, Blomfield had developed a taste for what he regarded as the old English tradition of garden design (it was actually more European, specifically Italian). This looked back to seventeenth- and early eighteenth-century examples, and reflected even earlier practices – walled enclosures, sculptures, summerhouses and bowers, topiary, paths and alleys, all related carefully by simple geometrical schemes. Naturalism had no place in such gardens; instead there was restraint combined with an open admission that the garden, like the house, was man-made and hence artificial. You could call it formal, and Blomfield did, although he seems to have been the first to apply the term in this way.

Judging from his surviving buildings, which tend to be large, ponderous, and quintessentially Edwardian, Blomfield was not an attractive architect (to me, anyway). But as a writer he sparkled. He had a keen polemical style and was particularly skilled at shaping an argument to suit himself. As a result, *The Formal Garden* is predictably well populated with straw men, which by the end of the book lie scattered across the battlefield in various stages of dismemberment.

For example, he posits an absolute distinction between what he calls 'landscape gardening' and 'formal gardening'. The landscape gardener, heir to the radical ideas of eighteenth-century designers like 'Capability' Brown and Humphry Repton, has no time for anything but 'Nature' (whatever that is). He tends to ignore the house and its setting in favour of ill-defined abstractions and, when pressed, will 'go off at a tangent about horticulture and hot-houses'. Even his allegiance to 'naturalness' is a sham: 'Instead of leaving nature alone, the landscapist is always struggling to make nature lend itself to his deceptions.' Why, here is that noted landscapist William Robinson contradictorily talking about 'quite second-rate types of vegetation'.

The formal gardener, on the other hand, accepts that a design 'depends for its success on the combined effect of house and garden'. Since you can't make the building resemble anything in nature ('unless you are content with a mud hut and cover it with grass'), you must 'so control and modify the grounds as to bring nature into harmony with the house'. After all, 'it is no more unnatural to clip a yew tree than to cut grass.'

As might be expected from a disciple of William Morris, many of Blomfield's arguments in favour of 'old-fashioned' gardens have a decidedly romantic tinge, as do the drawings by F. Inigo Thomas that illustrate it. Blomfield can write fetchingly of an out-of-date garden in a country town where you might find 'old-fashioned flowers against the red-brick wall and a broad stretch of velvety turf set off by ample paths of gravel, and at one corner, perhaps, a dainty summer-house of brick with marble floor and panelled sides; and all so quiet and sober'. Yet at the next moment, with a swipe of his rhetorical knife, he can be making fun of the Robinsonian tradition of basic horticultural skills: 'To plan out a garden the knowledge necessary is that of design, not the best method of growing a giant gooseberry.'

Much of *The Formal Garden* – the best part, really – is devoted to descriptions of old English formal gardens and their features: courts, terraces, walks, *parterres*, knots, garden architecture and much else – even fishponds. It is written with considerable scholarship for the time and with a real sense of pleasure in the subject. In spite of Blomfield's claim that the 'landscapists' had virtually swept the nineteenth-century gardening board, in the preceding twenty years the Arts and Crafts movement had actually stimulated a revival of interest in the formal style, which was especially suitable for smaller properties. Many readers apparently welcomed *The Formal Garden* as a kind of handbook, and it was to go into several editions.

William Robinson, however, saw it as something else. He saw it as a deliberate – and personal – attack on all he stood for, which was plenty. The situation was made worse by the fact that still another, though less important, book about formal gardens had just come out, by an architect named J. D. Sedding. Beside himself, Robinson delivered an infuriated riposte. It took the form of a small volume called *Garden Design and Architects' Gardens*, and its principal note was one of aggrieved defensiveness.

Reading this book, it is impossible not to feel twinges of sympathy for Robinson. Of course he manages a few telling blows against the state of English architecture ('In these days – when our ways of building are the laughing stock of all who care for beautiful buildings – there is plenty for the architect to do without spoiling our gardens') and Blomfield's high-handedness ('Mr Blomfield writes nonsense and then attributes it to me'). But for the most part he is never able to seize the initiative. Instead, he spends his energy denying accusations – that he ever attempted to 'reproduce uncultivated nature', or approved 'lawn-destruction by the terrace-builders and bedding-out gardeners', or 'ignored the house'. When he does go on the attack he is fatally lacking in precision. 'What is declared by Mr Blomfield to be absurd is the soul of true gardening – to show, on a small scale it may be, some of the precious and inexhaustible loveliness of vegetation on plain or wood or mountain.'

Blomfield must have been delighted. In a preface to the second edition of his book, happy to carry on 'a good scrap', he claimed that 'Mr Robinson's irritation had betrayed him into unnecessary blunders as well as gratuitous discourtesy.'

Whether this was true or not, the objective historian must admit that the fight was hardly a fair one or even, for that matter, waged between real opponents. After all, Robinson's own garden at Gravetye Manor had a number of formal features, including square beds surrounded by paving so that he could visit his favourite plants by wheelchair, and a magnificent pergola. As for Blomfield, according to Gertrude Jekyll, the garden he eventually built had 'not a straight line in it'. It cascaded down a cliff below Point Hill, his country house on the Sussex coast near Rye.

It was Jekyll who, with her usual good sense – and connections to both sides in the controversy, to Robinson in philosophy and to the formal school through her garden-design work with Lutyens – had a mediating word to offer. Writing in the *Edinburgh Review* in 1896, she regretted that the battle had 'taken on a somewhat bitter and personal tone . . . Both are right and both are wrong.' The formalists, 'architects to a man', have a point when they admire the dignity and beauty of the old gardens. But they make the mistake of ignoring 'the immense resources that are the precious possession of modern gardeners . . . We cannot go back a century or two and stop short . . .' It would be like stopping music with Bach, or painting with Botticelli.

With his book a success, Blomfield seems to have mellowed. In the preface to the third edition, in 1901, he graciously confessed that the time for polemics had passed, and that both formal gardens and wild gardens had value. In fact, 'the object of formal gardening is to bring the two into harmony'.

Robinson, typically unmollified, was still fussing years later, in print and in person. *The Garden Beautiful*, published in 1907, continued to complain about the formalists. And when a visitor seeing square beds at Gravetye exclaimed with surprise, 'Oh, why, *you* have a formal garden!' he retorted with all the old vigour. It was not the *shape* of the beds that offended, but the way they were planted, 'in geometrical designs, as in carpet gardening and bedding out'. Ironically, Blomfield – who had no more love for carpet bedding than Robinson did – would have agreed wholeheartedly.

LOST GARDENS

Mowing

I sometimes think that my main function as a gardener is mowing the lawn. I've been doing it long enough. A neighbour in Ypsilanti named Mrs Hole used to pay me a quarter for pushing an under-lubricated reel mower around her yard for about three hours, and I felt I was reasonably well paid, which should give you some idea of just how long. These days I have a tame young man to do the bulk of my mowing, but when a summer weekend goes by without firing up the machine myself, I still actually get jumpy, think of all that grass *growing*. At the moment I've got two lawn mowers, one a huge 22-inch Tuff-cut with big rear wheels and an engine large enough to propel a hearse, the other a zingy little blue Australian number that you have to push while listening to its two-cycle motor bang genteelly from time to time. I used to have a third mower, but a slightly proud lilac stump caused it to commit lawn-mower *seppuku* – a bent crankshaft and a blade that looked as though someone had tried to make a hairpin out of it. The vicissitudes of mowing.

You have a lot of time to think while you're mowing, which is one of the reasons I like it. Apart from deciding whether to go counter-clockwise (thereby throwing the clippings outward and spreading them all over the lawn) or clockwise (thus running *over* the clippings and either blowing them inward into an easy-to-rake heap or – more likely – clogging up the blade with what looks like green wallpaper paste), you have nothing to do but brood on the logic behind lawns and lawn mowers. Of which there isn't much, and probably never was. In the sixteenth century, when Francis Bacon made his famous observation that 'nothing is more pleasant to the eye than green grass finely shorn', the most common lawn mower by far was a sheep.

Despite William Robinson's claim that 'the lawn is the heart of the garden, and the happiest thing in it', the history of lawns, much less lawn mowers, is pretty sketchy. Pliny the Younger, in the first century AD, spoke of a *pratulum*, or 'little meadow', as a garden feature, without specifying whether the grass was long or short. The origin of the word 'lawn' itself is lost, along with much else, in the mists of ancient Celtic philology; it seems to be related to 'land', and to the Welsh *llan* ('enclosure', later 'church') that turns up as the unpronounceable first syllable of so many place-names in Wales. If we are to believe the old story about the American tourist who asked the gardener at a grand English house how he made the lawn look so nice, and was told that it was simple, you only had to mow it and roll it for about three hundred years, then lawns must go back at least to the seventeenth century. But this strikes me as improbable, if only because of the labour involved in mowing large expanses of grass closely with a scythe. And the fact is that men armed with scythes were the original lawn mowers, after the sheep.

I have used a scythe. I have watched people using scythes who knew what they were doing. I fully understand the principle of keeping the scythe razor-sharp and perfectly balanced, so as to minimize the expenditure of energy. But I still don't understand how you mow a lawn with a scythe. A hayfield, maybe, but not a lawn.

Until 1832, though, mowing a lawn meant scything it. First you rolled it. Then, a day or two later, early in the morning when the grass was still damp and soft, you mowed. A good man could manage about a quarter of an acre before 10 a.m., when the grass got too dry for the scythe to 'bite'. For a really good job, you'd also have to figure on two or three hours for a team of women to sweep up the cuttings with twig brooms. With an inexperienced mower you could expect 'circular sears, inequalities and bare patches ... which continue visible for several days'. Now this may not sound too bad compared with the havoc caused by a rotary power mower topping a molehill, but it must have been depressing, and it made the next development in lawn care all the more welcome.

About 1830 a foreman in a Gloucestershire cloth factory invented a machine to shear the nap on velvet, and then had the wit to realize that the same principle could be used in a machine to shear grass. He got a patent for it, noting (with admirable prescience) that 'country gentlemen may find, in using my machine themselves, an amusing, useful, and healthy exercise'. We are all in your debt, Edwin Beard Budding. In 1832 Ransome's began marketing a 19-inch version of the Budding machine, and soon dozens of sizes and designs were whirring, clattering and clanking around the British countryside. And, as one garden writer pointed out, the mower was likely to have a good reception 'in America and Australia, where manual labour is expensive and rare'.

These early machines had plenty of drawbacks. The biggest was simply getting them to move. They tended to be heavy and unwieldy, to say the least. A reader writing to the *Gardener's Chronicle* in 1868 suggested that 'it would be as well to purchase a boys' size for a man, while a ladies' size is probably best for a boy'. In 1842 Shanks patented a horse-drawn machine (the horse had to wear special boots to avoid scarring the greensward), while in the 1860s an American model, the Archimedean, offered the improvement of a single spiral blade. (This was a hit in England, where the normally chauvinistic magazine the *Field* declared it 'far superior to any of ours'.) Some people tried building their own to save money (Ransome's Budding machines cost a stiff 7 to 10 guineas in 1842); a man in Scotland assembled a large, pony-powered version capable of mowing 2½ acres in the same number of hours. For all the ingenuity expended, however, most of the mowers available in these early years were, as the *Gardener's Chronicle* put it, 'cumbrous heavy things that made a maximum of ear-torturing sound, entailed severe labour to work and much difficulty to regulate'.

Unsurprisingly, conservatives were not slow to complain. Noise from the cogwheels, linking wheels and blades caused considerable fuss ('When visitors have stepped in at the house the machine has to be stopped, because of the annoyance!'), and the scythe still had its adherents. 'As a regular reader and gardener,' harrumphed one letter-writer to a gardening magazine, 'allow me to protest against the way in which the buyer of a lawn mower is deceived if he purchases (per advert.) a 16-inch machine to be worked easily by one man. He finds that it takes two instead of one . . . I have been three times deceived . . . I prefer the labour of using a scythe to that of working a 16-inch mower.' In 1850 the *Chronicle* solemnly recommended using *both* mower and scythe: 'In wet weather, on moist soils, it is almost impossible to get the machine to work well, whilst in droughts it is nearly as difficult to make the scythe cut the grass.'

Nevertheless, expert scythesmen were a dying breed, and more and more thought was going into building better machines. In 1858 a mower made by Green cut 1,600 square feet in 6 minutes, 35 seconds, to win a competition; at the Paris International Exhibition in 1889 the Perfected Pennyslvania, an American design looking pretty much like the one I pushed in 1940, took a silver medal. They were still tough to use. As late as 1924 a gardening manual was still repeating the familiar refrain: 'A 10-inch machine is quite enough for a man, or up to a 12- or 14-inch size for a man and a boy.' The main thing lacking, in fact, was *power*, and that came next.

In 1893, accompanied by a cloud of smoke and the sound of hissing, Leyland's magnificent steam mower lumbered on to the field, an exemplary representative of the age of dreadnoughts. It weighed 1½ tons fully armed and, according to one observer, 'not unexpectedly suffered from lack of manoeuvrability'. The operator, who steered from behind, had to contend with soot, cinders and, presumably, a certain constant nervousness about inadvertently levelling hedges, small trees and fellow gardeners. Attaching a seat and control gear turned out to be an extremely modest improvement. But this didn't matter, because before long steam was obsolete too. In 1902 Ransome's introduced the first petrol-powered mower.

Ninety years later most of us take mowers pretty much for granted, which is fair enough; a turn around the lawn once a week keeps things under control. There are interesting local variations, of course. A mower doesn't get much use in Hong Kong, for example. Our gardener there used to spend whole days squatting on the lawn, prodding out weeds, and never mowed at all. And then there is the matter of *stripes*. Until I moved to England, I confess that my interest in stripes was minimal. Here you can't avoid them.

The typical English mowing machine, say a Suffolk Punch, the kind you'd use on a weedless, croquet-smooth, 300-year-old English lawn, is a reel mower and tends to be fairly heavy, with a weighty roller in back and a grass-catcher perched up front.

Trundling in a straight line across the lawn, the roller presses down the cut grass in one direction going, and the other direction coming back. Result: stripes. Even rotary mowers over here are made so as to leave stripes, or they are regarded as slacking the job.

This stripe fixation has one serious consequence. The standard English lawn mower doesn't work very well on the standard lawn – that is, a lawn with bumps which may not get mowed two or three times a week. In my ignorance, I bought one, thinking that with a classical English lawn mower I could have a classical English lawn. The ad, I remember, praised 'our latest piece of wizardry: a rotary mower that can turn a shagpile into an Axminster'. Those are carpets, I recognized, enchanted by the idea of combining the slash power of a rotary with the finesse of a reel and ending up with stripes. At the first small bump, however, the mower faltered, and when it hit a clump of goosegrass it stopped dead. Thanks to a kindly dealer, I was able to exchange it for the little blue Australian two-cycle, which not only lacks pretension but features an ingenious disk on the business end with two small pivoting blades loosely bolted to it. You can hit anything short of a tombstone and no serious damage ensues. Of course, it is not wheel-powered, which would be awfully nice. No stripes, either.

The ride-on mower, I'm happy to report, has not come to Britain in significant numbers yet. It may not be long in coming, however, judging from a television commercial shown here last summer. An ancient gardener, clearly past his prime, is invited into the house for a word with the master. Old Tusser is sure (and so are we) that he's going to get the sack because he no longer has the energy to stripe the lawn properly. But no! The master has bought a spanking-new ride-on mower! There it is, sitting out on the polished green lawn, just waiting for Tusser to clamber aboard! A thankful, doglike smile creases the ancient cheeks; tears well up in the rheumy eyes. Sniffs of proprietary sympathy all around as the master, his wife and Old Tusser gaze at the machine in profound satisfaction. Nobody has bothered to explain to Tusser yet how he is supposed to navigate around that serpentine herbaceous border.

On the other hand, maybe it doesn't matter. The British have always had an affection for mowing machines. How many other countries can boast an Old Lawnmower Club, or a Lawnmower Museum? The latter, located in an attic in Southport, Lancashire, boasts 100 machines, all in working order. (The fact that the museum's proprietor has 200 more waiting to be fixed, by the way, strikes me as entirely appropriate. Waiting to be fixed is a natural state of existence for lawn mowers.) Strictly for the love of it – old mowers go cheap – club members delight in exploring derelict garden sheds in hopes of turning up a 1926 22-inch Atco with a brass flywheel, a 1903 Green steam-powered job, or perhaps even an authentic early Budding (only four examples known). Then the challenge is to get the thing to run.

My own contribution to British enlightenment is the 22-inch Tuff-cut mower I imported when I moved over here. It is only slightly more manoeuvrable than Leyland's steam machine, but it has power on its impressively large rear wheels (one of which is now disconcertingly yellow; the only replacement tyre I could find was from a child's bike) and can chop through everything growing in my lawn, including oak seedlings. It may be a bit rough for your English gardener, a little too coarse in its workings, a touch brash and, well, *American*. But walking behind it, listening to the muffled rumble of all those six horsepower, watching and smelling the cut grass spew fragrantly out of the side, I can't help but feel some faint spiritual kinship with the men with scythes who came before me, and who probably also wondered more than once whether there was really any sense in making lawns and mowing them.

Water Jokes

As every parent knows, the surest way to entertain a four-year-old on an uncomfortably hot summer's day is to turn on a garden hose and let him squirt everything in sight, including himself and probably you. We've all done it; it's simple-minded, and a lot of fun for everybody involved. Water is like that – it can make you laugh.

But so far as water in gardens is concerned, I'm afraid, we have rather lost our sense of humour. We certainly don't lack for grandeur, graciousness or beauty, and these are, without question, vastly worthy objectives. One has only to think of the water 'eye' at Longwood Gardens, near Wilmington in Delaware, ceaselessly, shimmeringly, yet almost imperceptibly, overflowing, or the lake at Stourhead in Devon, brilliant with reflections in the autumn; or Brazilian designer Roberto Burle Marx's elegant formal pools bristling with jungle plants. All impressive, indeed. But fun? Not exactly.

A trip to Granada in southern Spain a few weeks ago gave rise to these thoughts. We went to the Alhambra – in fact, we stayed on the Alhambra Hill, in a one-time convent that has now been turned into an extremely pleasant hotel – to see the gardens and palaces of the Moorish kings. The Alhambra is a wonderfully watery place, especially when you think of how dry the surrounding country is. As you climb up the winding road through the woods to the palace-topped summit, a thunderous cascade emerges from beneath the walls before swirling off (invisibly) through underground conduits to rejoin the Rio Darro whence it came. This is merely the overflow, the surplus. More water fills the pools in the royal gardens and variously trickles or splashes in the fountains. The very sound of it is cooling. It's easy to understand why Mohammad ben Al-Ahmar, the Moorish ruler of this little kingdom in the thirteenth century, with arid generations of North African desert-dwellers in his psyche, must have delighted in it. A lot easier, in fact, than to grasp the degree of engineering skill required to re-route an entire river 8 miles through mountains in order to provide a constant flow at an altitude hundreds of feet above the plain.

The Moorish use of water in the Alhambra strikes a particularly joyful note, as if sheer abundance is itself cause for pleasure. The most charming – if not the most spectacular – part of the complex is the small summer palace called the Generalife, perched among cypresses and arcaded walks on a hill opposite the main buildings. Here you get an especially strong feeling that to the people who laid out and lived in these pavilions and gardens, water was something to play with. The long pool in the Court of the Canal, for example, is today bordered by rows of nozzles endlessly squirting water in wobbling, chuckling arcs that mostly land in the pool, but just as often splash the stone paving and the shrubs growing in big pots alongside. The effect is whimsical. Even more whimsical – whimsy raised to a kind of art – is the flight of stairs called the Camino de los Cascades in the upper garden, whose banisters are actually narrow troughs filled with running water. I call that splendid.

The real heyday of water play in the garden was in sixteenth-century Italy. In fact, they even had a name for it – *giochi d'acqua*, meaning 'water games' or (better) 'water jokes'. Most of the truly spectacular examples have long since dried up, but a few drawings and sketches survive. More vivid are the accounts of foreign travellers, particularly the great French essayist Montaigne and the Englishman John Evelyn. Both men seem to have been fascinated, if not obsessed, by the tricks that could be played with water. Their journals are full of amazement.

In 1580, for example, Montaigne visited the just completed gardens of Villa Pratolino, the estate near Florence created for Francesco de' Medici, Grand Duke of Tuscany. The designer of the gardens was Bernardo Buontalenti, who on the strength of this work alone must be classed as one of the greatest hydraulic engineers of all time; he built an aqueduct 3 miles long and filled the place with an array of fountains, cascades, watercourses and pools. More than that, he showed how much fun water could be. Here is Montaigne (or rather his secretary, who was keeping notes at this point in the journey):

There is one miraculous thing, a grotto with several cells and rooms ... There is not only music and harmony made by the movement of the water, but also a movement of several statues and doors of various actions, caused by the water; several animals that plunge in to drink; and things like that. At one single movement the whole grotto is full of water, and all the seats squirt water on your buttocks; and if you flee from the grotto and climb the castle stairs, and anyone takes pleasure in this sport, there come out of every other step of the stairs, right up to the top of the house, a thousand jets of water that give you a bath.

The grotto at Pratolino, known as the 'garden of marvels', seems to have had the whole range of water jokes – musical devices, water-powered moving figures and tricks to play on the unsuspecting. Water played other roles too, of course; in 1645

John Evelyn reported going down 'a large Walk, at the sides whereof gushed out of imperceptible pipes, couched under- neath, slender pissings of water, that interchangeably fell into each others Chanells, making a lofty and perfect arch, so as a man on horseback may ride under it and not be wet one drop'. Pratolino's only surviving original feature is a watery one, the gigantic statue of a shaggy bearded figure (variously called 'Appenine' or 'Neptune') who is squatting on a hillside appar- ently squeezing a cascade out of the mouth of a fish-like monster.

In Florence, at another of the Grand Duke's palaces, Mon- taigne found 'a rocky structure in the form of a pyramid' contain- ing 'water mills and windmills, little church bells, soldiers of the guard, animals, hunts, and a thousand such things', all of which started clacking, spinning and ringing when the *fontanniere* turned on the water. Mere movement was not enough. There were also sound effects. A number of gardens featured hydraulic aviaries, in which water-driven bellows produced convincing bird- songs while fake birds hopped on fake branches. The Villa d'Este in Tivoli went one better, Evelyn noted. Its aviary boasted an artificial owl, and when the owl suddenly appeared, all the other birds fell silent – 'to the admiration of the Spectators'.

No doubt because Italy is a warm and sunny place, a typical water joke usually involved a surprise drenching. Visiting Cardi- nal Aldobrandini's villa at Frascati, reported a dripping Evelyn, 'one can hardly step without wetting to the skin'. A favourite device was a stone table and stone benches fitted with hidden spray pipes, so that a too solemn banquet could be enlivened by the turn of a tap. Pratolino had one, and an example still exists in the sixteenth-century garden of Hellbrunn near Salzburg. Given the difference in climate, the latter must have been challenging.

Still more complicated arrangements for getting visitors wet amused Montaigne at the Villa Medici in Castello. His secretary described the scene:

For as they were walking about the garden and looking at its curiosities, the gardener left the company for this purpose; and as they were in a certain spot contemplating certain marble statues, there spurted under their feet and between their legs, through an infinite number of tiny holes, jets of water so minute that they were almost invisible, imitating supremely well the trickle of fine rain, with which they were completely sprinkled by the operation of some underground spring which the gardener was working from more than two hundred paces from there, with such artifice that from there on the outside he made these spurts of water rise and fall as he pleased, turning and moving them just as he wanted.

Such marvels! Palisades of water springing up from the earth, a marble table 'on which a fountaine plays in divers forms of glasses, cupps, crosses, fanns, crownes &c.', mythological scenes completely animated 'by the force of Water', storms that could be turned on and off ('which such a fury of raine, wind and Thunder that one would imagine oneself in some extreame Tempest'), stone musketeers shooting visitors unexpectedly with streams of water, crowns and copper balls bouncing miraculously in mid-air on waterspouts, hydraulic organs playing music all by themselves – no wonder visitors were impressed. If they were rich enough, they went home and ordered imitations. Italian experts scattered over Europe to supply the engineering know-how. Henri IV brought Tommaso Francini and his two brothers to France, where they reproduced some of the features of Pratolino in Henri's lavish gardens at Saint-Germain-en-Laye. In England Henry VIII built waterworks at his palace of Nonsuch, and Elizabeth I is supposed to have had a trick fountain at Hampton Court 'to play upon the ladies and others standing by, and give them a thorough wetting'.

One English grotto replete with water jokes achieved almost the fame of its Italian predecessors. Isaac de Caus, a Dutch engineering genius, designed the gardens of Wilton House for the Fourth Earl of Pembroke in the 1630s, and when Celia Fiennes visited the grotto there forty years or so later, this is what she found:

In the middle roome is a round table, a large pipe in the midst, on which they put a crown or gun or a branch, and so it spouts the water through the carvings and poynts all round the roome at the Artists pleasure to wet the Company . . . on each side is two little roomes which by the turning their wires the water runnes in the rockes you see and hear it, and also it is so contrived in one room that it makes the melody of Nightingerlls and all sorts of birds which engaged the curiosity of the Strangers to go in to see, but at the entrance off each room, is a line of pipes that appear not till by a sluce moved it washes the spectators, designed for diversion.

Perhaps because of plumbing problems – we must assume that at some point the taps started to seize up and the pipes to leak – or a simple change in taste, in time water jokes like these apparently went out of fashion. In 1733 the ninth Earl 'destroyed the old rediculous Water works and whims' at Wilton, while in 1819 Villa Pratolino itself suffered transmogrification into, of all things, an 'English garden'. The use of water had ceased to be playful. An odd gimmick or two lingered on – Chatsworth has a metal tree with sprays of water in place of branches. But by the end of the seventeenth century, particularly in the hands of the great French designer le Nôtre, water in the garden had become a far more serious affair, a matter of elegance and proportion and sophistication with no interest in squirting people or making artificial birds sing. In some ways I can't help but think this a loss – perhaps a loss of innocence.

While it's unlikely that we shall soon see a return to hydraulic organs in our gardens, it would be foolish to conclude that other kinds of water playfulness are gone forever. The English designer Geoffrey Jellicoe – now in his nineties, and still at work – produced an ingenious musical cascade at Shute House in Dorset, where each tiny waterfall in the series produces a different note. Admittedly, it won't squirt you, but in my view it's a step in the right direction.

Bedding Out

As everybody knows, it is Gertrude Jekyll (and her unfairly less well-known colleague and editor William Robinson) whose gardening ideas hold almost universal sway these days. Herbaceous borders billowing with subtly modulated colours, hardy plants in and for their natural forms, walls and paths and water deliberately integrated with unrestrained vegetation, a romantic (and generally labour-saving) attitude towards design – all these are now virtually taken for granted, whatever permutations a gardener or planner may invent. It is easy to forget, in such circumstances, that this particular approach was, in fact, a major departure a century ago. Then, few people felt much nostalgia – or admiration – for the classic cottage garden filled with roses, phloxes, foxgloves and clouds of forget-me-nots. Cottage gardens didn't show off 'the art of the gardener' and were altogether too messy for a newly mechanized era. Jekyll and Robinson were revolutionaries. But what were they revolting against?

It was in search of an answer to this interesting, if unimperative, question that I went trawling through a large stack of old gardening books and magazines the other day, and I am happy to report that what I came upon was as revolting as anyone could wish – *bedding out*. Given the nature of bedding out at its peak of popularity, it is easy to see why most historians of gardening tend to leap, as if embarrassed, straight from the great landscape designers of the eighteenth century (such as William Kent and 'Capability' Brown) to Robinson, whose 1883 book *The English Flower Garden* first set forth many principles of the modern style. But bedding out is too odd to be ignored.

For a succinct description of the system, we may turn to the 1844 edition of *The Ladies' Companion to the Flower Garden* by Jane Loudon, a popular handbook offering instruction, in the most intimidating detail, on growing everything from mushrooms to the toothache tree. Beds, explained Mrs Loudon, are 'divisions of a flower-garden, which are formed in different figures, and which are generally covered with a mass of flowers of one kind, or at least of one colour, though they sometimes contain single plants, or small tufts of plants or flowers, at regular distances, with naked spaces showing the soil between'. She might have gone on to say (and no doubt would have, if she hadn't run out of subordinate clauses) that in its mature form the bedding system – also known as the 'massing system' – aimed at producing a continuous display of brightly coloured blooms and foliage laid out in more or less intricate two-dimensional patterns. Never a dull moment was the ideal. The zingier the colour, the more spectacular the display, the more complicated the figures, the more, well, *plants*, the better.

Bedding seems to have been an outgrowth of *parterre*, the geometrical layout of low plants, edging, gravel and bare earth that achieved its most grandiose expression in France on the vast prairies of Versailles and Vaux-le-Vicomte. Domesticated versions of *parterre* had been a feature of gardens, greater and lesser, for a long time; for that matter, the notion of a garden as a mere decorated surface is a very ancient one. But a combination of factors early in the nineteenth century apparently brought on the bloom in bedding. Primary among them was the influence of the landscape designer Humphry Repton who, unlike Kent and Brown, had no objection to introducing shrubs and flowers into his schemes. He considered a large extent of empty 'dressed ground' to be rather melancholy. Moreover, Repton had an audience different from his predecessors' — instead of ducal clients, he spoke to the comfortably well-off owners of villas and small estates, who had to be satisfied with a few acres of what Repton called 'embellished neatness' rather than square miles of vistas and parkland. The alteration in scale presented fresh opportunities for display. What better way to consume conspicuously?

It is no easier to pin down just who was responsible for the invention of bedding than to lay the blame for the excesses that gradually took over. Repton himself never spoke of the practice as such, merely commenting that 'flower gardens on a small scale may, with propriety, be formal and artificial; but in all cases require neatness and attention.' One theory holds that the idea of massing plants for colour was first put into effect at Lord Grenville's estate of Dropmore in Buckinghamshire in the 1820s. Another key date is 1829, when John Robson, head gardener at Linton, discovered that the ultimate bedding plants, pelargoniums, could be made to grow outdoors. What is certain is that by the time of Victoria's accession in 1837, the newly prosperous were eagerly vying with each other (and the old money) to see who could manage to grow the most plants and bed them out the most intricately.

A new aesthetic came into existence. Family initials, heraldic devices, monograms and all manner of floral curlicues and doo-dads began appearing on formerly chaste lawns. The best authorities proclaimed that beds should be placed symmetrically, and contain only plants of a certain height so as to maintain the two-dimensional effect. The demand for continuous bloom meant constant attention from a substantial gardening staff – pinching back, deadheading, sprucing up, sometimes (as a disapproving writer noted in Robinson's magazine the *Garden*) 'working a kind of bridge to enable them to get into the beds'. Complete replanting had to take place several times in a summer, with hundreds of spare plants kept in the reserve ground to fill any gaps. You could judge a man's standing, so the saying went, by the number of his bedding plants: 10,000 for a squire, 20,000 for a baronet, 30,000 for an earl, and so on. Trollope neglects to tell us how many the Duke of Omnium had – at least 100,000, probably!

Besides the pelargoniums, what exactly were the plants? Certainly not the old English favourites like snapdragons and hollyhocks and columbines; they were too tall, or flowered irregularly, or sprawled. More exciting – and in some cases more demanding – were the exotic new tender perennials reaching Europe from South Africa and Central and South America: calceolarias, begonias, lantanas, fuchsias, coleuses. Such plants provided an excellent excuse for building acres of fancy greenhouses and hiring regiments of gardeners. Then there were lobelias, marigolds, centaureas, dianthuses, pyrethrums, verbenas, pansies, alternantheras, echeverias. Amaranthus came highly recommended for its foliage, though the two most interesting sorts – *Amaranthus tricolor* and *A. elegantissimus* – tended to come up plain green, so you had to pot three for every two needed. Bulbs by the hundreds and thousands filled the beds in the springtime. But these were scarcely the end of it. For a gardener blessed with extra time (unlikely), or an extra-large staff, almost anything could be employed for bedding out, and was – roses (carefully pegged down so that stems and leaves did not show), clematises (likewise), even delphiniums (though the pegging down was pointedly described by one writer as 'a nice business . . . no one should employ delphiniums as bedding plants until confident of the capacity to perform this operation without breaking the stems').

Sub-tropical plants remained fashionable and got a boost in 1845 when the British government took the tax off glass. (Greenhouses were essential both for growing such plants in bedding quantities and for keeping them healthy until the weather was warm enough to set them out.) Until then, glass had been taxed by weight, which induced manufacturers to make it as thin as possible and in turn made roofing a hot-house a nightmare. Big panes were simply too fragile, and even small panes could be shattered in a hailstorm or punctured by a disoriented bird. The thin glass had to be overlapped to keep out the cold, which meant that it also kept out most of the light whenever a crop of 'minute confervae' (that is to say, green slime) grew in the water that collected between the panes. Relieved of the tax, overly enthusiastic gardeners promptly switched to thick slabs of plate glass 2 or 3 feet long and a foot wide. These merely bent the greenhouse frames and – being too clear – scorched the plants most depressingly. In time, however, they got it right. Glasshouse architecture (and bedding plants) flourished, culminating in the biggest glass-house of all, Joseph Paxton's gigantic Crystal Palace, the hit of the 1851 International Exhibition. Paxton, of course, was a gardener.

With the fad for bedding out in full swing, the American gardening writer A. J. Downing praised 'the *Modern* or *English* flower garden', saying that 'there cannot be a question that this method of planting . . . is productive of by far the most splendid effect.' Municipal gardeners all over Europe and North America filled parks with ever more glaring and meticulous displays, spending huge amounts of public money creating marigold mottoes and coleus cusps, adorning train stations and making cemeteries gay, constructing floral clocks that actually told the time. A Mr Mason, superintendent of Princes Park, Liverpool, invented 'tessellated colouring . . . the colours being repeated in small blotches, with sharp dividing lines to separate the groups . . . thus creating a rich mosaic or tessellated pattern extremely interesting and pleasing' but 'rather wanting in decidedness'. Decisive effects were important. To achieve them there were parquet beds; scrolls and ribbons; panel gardens with geometric colouring, hearts, diamonds, horns of plenty and lovers' knots; and beds 'thrown together in groups and constellations, as stars are in a firmament'.

It couldn't last. Beginning in the first issues of his new magazine the *Garden*, which he launched in 1871, William Robinson fulminated against bedding out. After reprinting an innocent lecture by a Yorkshire parson named C. P. Peach, in which the practice was defended for spreading a love of flowers among 'so many of the lower orders', Robinson blasted away at 'the evils of the system', and complacently noted that 'there can be no doubt whatever that except in the most benighted of places, a considerable reduction of summer bedding has been witnessed'. After all, he maintained, 'it is the worst gardening ever introduced, and the sooner it is changed the better'.

Now the anti-bedders joined in mercilessly. 'Cakes upon a pastrycook's tray,' they complained. 'Makes one think of a farthing kaleidoscope'; 'a poor, gingerbread entity'; 'hateful gyrations, which place the art of gardening on a level so much lower than it deserves to occupy'; 'finniking beds'; and so on. Shirley Hibberd, another leading gardening editor, spoke with horror of 'bedding plants . . . exposed on a great treeless, turfless place like a blazing fire at the mouth of a coal-pit'. Soon Gertrude Jekyll, who started writing for Robinson's magazine in 1875, joined the chorus. Even William Morris, whom nobody asked, called carpet bedding 'an aberration of the human mind' and said, 'I blush with shame.' Against such an onslaught, the defenders ('It may be formal, it may be vulgar in its glaring colours, but at least it gives you flowers you can see') sounded increasingly unconvincing. Quite apart from the *diktats* of the authorities, bedding was proving itself to be a terrible nuisance. One poor rector with eighteen beds to fill confessed in 1863 that ten years of 'Geranium fever of a very scarlet type' had left him for seven months a year with 'laundry full, study windows full, dressing room ditto, and if I go down into my cellar I hit my head against Tom Thumbs hung down from the ceiling'.

Today, on the great estates of Britain, troops of gardeners no longer labour into the night striking cuttings of calceolaria. The fashion now, if one is to have glass, is for a conservatory where you can raise your tender plants and then sit among them on a sunny Sunday morning, perhaps sipping coffee and eating an orange. But bedding has not quite passed into oblivion. It has changed, admitting greater flexibility in design and planting. I was delighted to see, for example, that each of the brilliant beds in front of the Thames Water Authority offices in London last summer featured two or three stalks of sweet corn in its centre. Such garden writers as Christopher Lloyd and Rosemary Verey still find a good word to say for bedding. Certain municipal authorities still find cash to pay for it. Boston, for example, maintains its Public Garden beds. Edinburgh keeps up its famous floral clock, along with a quantity of bedding bright enough to stand out even in ceaseless rain. And in London's Victoria Embankment Gardens, beds are faithfully cleared, dug and replanted several times a year with spring bulbs, wall- flowers, pelargoniums, zinnias, verbenas, petunias, salvias, centaureas and purple-leafed beets, all massed in patterns. I have to admit that it looks pretty good. And you *can* see the flowers without squinting.

Retrieving the Past

It occurred to me the other day that gardening is the only art form I can think of that works in four dimensions – that is, the usual three, plus time. Time shapes the garden and completes it; it also, in the end, destroys it. Any gardener has to be aware of what the passage of time will mean in terms of fulfilling a plan (is the kolkwitzia going to swamp the magnolia? How long before the beech hedge matures?), but most of us, I suspect, would prefer not to think too much about the destruction part.

Maybe we shouldn't despair. Given the proper degree of enthusiasm (and sufficient funds), even seriously time-compromised gardens can be retrieved from oblivion. They need not necessarily vanish in a maze of brush and saplings, or be overplanted with shopping centres. In some cases – rare enough, I admit – they can throw a challenge in the teeth of time and show themselves in something like their original splendour of two or three hundred years ago.

This is the province of the garden restorer, a sort of combination historian-horticulturist-connoisseur with a taste for ancient tradesman's bills, plant lists, household accounts, reports from long-ago tourists, paintings and sketches (frequently inartistic) and the latest aerial photographs. Out of this gallimaufry of data he (or often she) can sometimes recover what to most of us would seem hopelessly lost, and even recreate it – not as a plastic fragment of Disneyland, but in the form of a real garden as alive, moving and authentic as the original.

To anybody who cares about the past, and is curious to know how people felt and acted in circumstances remote from our own, this enterprise has a peculiar value. Beyond retrieving a chunk of history you can actually walk around in – no small feat in itself – it offers us a chance to experience at first hand how a garden actually *worked*. The best way to explain what I mean may be to describe two restored gardens we visited recently, both dating from the first half of the eighteenth century and located within 8 miles of each other, yet totally different in almost every way: design, aesthetic style and effect on the visitor.

The first is Westbury Court Garden, begun in 1696 by Maynard Colchester, the scion of a wealthy family that owned estates in the flat, rich water meadows at the head of the Severn estuary, not far from Gloucester. Their money came largely from timber holdings in the Forest of Dean, and plenty of it had gone into building a fine house; now, having married a daughter of the Lord Mayor of London, Maynard wanted an equally fine garden. No doubt influenced in part by the nature of the setting – level and wet – he decided upon a formal Dutch water garden, with a long, stone-framed pool or 'canal', clipped yew hedges, walls, *parterres* set about with small trees cut into geometric shapes, and several pavilions, one an elegant two-storey affair from which you could gaze down and appreciate the overall pattern while taking tea or a light collation. No one knows who designed Colchester's garden – it may even have been a Dutchman, since many of the details, like the huge sash windows in the summerhouse, are purely Dutch. But, thanks to the survival of Maynard Colchester's personal account book, we do know an amazing amount about just how the garden was built, who the workmen were, what it was planted with and how much it all cost. This knowledge would come in handy 300 years later.

But time passed. Maynard's son, Maynard II, succeeded his father in 1715, improving the garden with another canal, 'T'-shaped this time. Other additions were a small, square, walled garden and a handsome stone gazebo. Maynard II also tore down the old house and built a new one, completing it in 1748. By then, however, the garden was hopelessly out of date and old-fashioned, probably a bit of an embarrassment. Certainly it was allowed to go downhill. The *parterres* had gone by 1785, according to a survey of that date, and in 1805 the family decided to demolish Westbury Court for its materials and move to another house some miles away. The garden was maintained in a desultory fashion, but except for a few years before World War I, nobody seems to have paid much attention to it. (In those days, the declining family fortunes were briefly restored by the advent of money from the royal house of Siam, when the splendidly named Maynard Willoughby Colchester-Wemyss assumed the guardianship of several of the crown princes being educated in England.) But by the time a speculator picked up the property in 1960, the garden was almost lost. Weeds choked the stagnant canals, the tall pavilion was half collapsed, the unclipped hedges were shapeless mounds. Nettles and brambles obscured all else. If the new buyer had had his way, the canals would have been filled with rubble and the site used to build ten houses.

In 1964, something close to a miracle happened. The local government took over Westbury Court, built a home for elderly people where the house used to be and gave the garden to the National Trust. By now it was a rarity, one of the very few seventeenth-century Dutch gardens left in England or even, for that matter, in Holland. There had been dozens once, but the great landscape architects of the eighteenth century like 'Capability' Brown saw to it that they were swept away as outmoded.

Restoration began in 1967. The tall pavilion had to be dismantled and rebuilt from the ground up; the great west wall that had bordered Maynard Colchester's canal, demolished by the speculator (who never got much farther with his projected ten houses), was not only reconstructed but planted with old varieties of espalier fruit trees – Lemon Pippin, Royal Russet, Nonpareil and Golden Reinette apples; Jargonelle and Beurre Brown pears; Green Gage and Fotheringham plums. Volunteers grubbed out the nettles and brambles and helped to replace the ancient yew hedges, some of which had drowned in floods, while the roots of others were penetrating and pulling apart the stone canal walls. Dredging the canals was a huge job – more than 1,000 cubic yards of silt had to be removed and spread over the eastern part of the garden.

Most surviving ancient gardens are a sort of palimpsest, a manuscript upon which successive generations have written and rewritten their new and often contradictory ideas. Getting back to the original can be an almost impossible challenge. In the case of Westbury Court, scarcely altered in 350 years, the problem was less severe, but the restorers were still lucky in having two wonderful sources to fall back on for information. The first was those detailed estate and personal account books in which Maynard Colchester set forth just how much each new bit of his garden cost as it was being built. On 10 September 1698, for example, he paid Thomas Wintle £15 7s. for laying 87,850 bricks – could that have been the west wall? There are payments to the 'weederwoman'; to nurserymen for trees and shrubs (cherries, 'filbeards', 'perimyd [pyramid]' hollies and yews, tuberoses, a 'red sweet water grape'); to masons for the stonework of the canal. We even find him paying 'Coz. Colchester' for hundreds of crocus, hyacinth, anemone and tulip bulbs. On the strength of such lists as these, and their knowledge of plant history, the restorers have been able to recreate a garden that Maynard himself would rejoice in.

Their other major aid was a picture. In about 1707, a Dutchman named Johannes Kip paid a call at Westbury Court. He was engaged in preparing, together with his fellow countryman Leonard Knyff, a volume of bird's-eye views of English estates to be called *Britannia Illustrata*, for sale mainly to those prosperous gentlemen whose houses were included. Kip was impressively accurate – perhaps the watery nature of the Westbury gardens made him feel at home. For here in his drawing, shown with great exactitude, are the *parterres*, the long rows of lollipop-shaped trees, the spirals and pyramids of clipped yews and hollies rising above the squared hedges, the placid canal and the tall pavilion with its pillared loggia at the base. The highway, of course, is rutted earth instead of Tarmac; and today the Elizabethan house is gone. But, looking at Kip's picture, you cannot doubt for a moment that this is indeed what Westbury Court was like then and, amazingly, is like today – formal, stately, enormously peaceful, satisfying one's instincts for spaciousness and closure at the same time. There is a hint of grandiosity; you can see how in the hands of the more megalomaniacal French such garden geometry could become vast and bleak. But here the scale is still human, still Dutch.

Across the Severn estuary, where the hills first start to rise out of the valley meadows, is a very different sort of restoration. What is now called Painswick Rococo Garden was built in the 1740s by Benjamin Hyett to accompany his newly constructed mansion, a rather severe classical edifice faced with the typical tan, cut Cotswold stone. In a departure from standard practice, however, Hyett made no attempt to tie the house and garden together but instead decided to make use of a deep cleft or combe a couple of hundred yards from the house, which you come upon only after passing through a gate in a high wall. The ground suddenly falls away in front of you, and beyond the trees – hazy in the autumn sunlight the day we were there – the combe opens to reveal lawns, alleys of yew hedging, a huge vegetable garden criss-crossed with grassed paths, a smooth bowling green and a wide rectangular pool at its foot. There is a semblance of geometric order, but even before you descend the winding path and begin to notice the various garden buildings – 'Gothick' pavilions, garden seats in various styles, a strange white curved structure with pointed arches and spires – it becomes clear that formality here has a function very different from the formality of Westbury Court. It is something to play with, or against; less a governing factor than a kind of implied joke.

Painswick had no easier time of it over the centuries than Westbury Court but never quite disappeared. The buildings progressively collapsed, and the valley floor came to harbour mostly vegetables and soft fruit. Still, until 1955 five gardeners were employed to take care of it. By 1965, however, the owner Richard Dickinson decided it was all too much and planted the whole combe with trees. It turned into a jungle, full of brambles and wild clematis.

Nearly twenty years later, having recognized the rarity of his garden – there are no other surviving gardens from the rococo period, roughly 1720 to 1760 – and the fact that someone turned up a careful 1748 painting of the original garden by Thomas Robins (who may actually have designed it in the first place), Lord Dickinson decided to undertake its restoration. He bulldozed the new wood, regraded the ground, had the ponds drained and their stonework repaired. Archaeologists figured out the location of paths and the details of vanished buildings, while experts in eighteenth-century horticulture gradually replaced the hedges and plantings. Work still goes on, funded by entrance fees and money from a charitable trust.

There is an air of good humour and jollity about Painswick. The garden buildings – stage-set-like, scarcely serious or even permanent in some cases – contribute much to this, and so does the way the fenced central beds are arranged on the slope, carefully but somehow comfortably, as if the geometrician had forgotten his squared paper but didn't care. Similarly, while you are conscious of art in the placement of the paths – the Beech Walk, the trails that wander around the old woods to an octagonal pigeon house to a strange little pavilion with an asymmetrical façade, through a grove where a mass of snowdrops bloom in the spring – it is an art that has begun to accept and enjoy the unpredictability of nature. Where Westbury Court has quiet stability, Painswick has spontaneity and adventurousness.

A good garden historian could no doubt point out to us the reasons for the contrast between these two gardens. The forty years that divide them had seen the beginnings of a whole new sensibility develop. But while I find this fascinating, I am still more struck by the fact that right now at the end of the twentieth century, we are able to return to the eighteenth century for an afternoon to see – and feel – the change for ourselves. No book can quite convey the emotional effect of the black yew hedges reflected in Maynard Colchester's long, stately canal, of the sparkling insouciance of Painswick's pink-and-white Eagle House pavilion, of the musk roses clambering over an old stone gate at Westbury Court. In them the past actually lives.

Ha! Ha!

When I was in Edinburgh in the 1950s, I started collecting books. In those days you could pick up a remarkable range of eighteenth-century volumes for a few shillings each, most of them in their original bedraggled bindings with a bookplate from some great, decayed private library. I bought Alexander Pope, a lot of James Boswell and Samuel Johnson, a slew of minor poetry and a splendid set of Horace Walpole's *Anecdotes of Painting in England* in quarto, its pages still as crisp and fresh inside their cracked covers as when they were printed at Horry's own Strawberry Hill Press in 1785.

At the time I cared nothing about gardening and knew less. This fact may explain (if not excuse) why I didn't realize until recently that I possessed a copy of one of the more famous documents of garden history. For, hidden at the end of the fourth volume of the *Anecdotes*, closely following an entry devoted to William Kent, was Walpole's classic essay 'On Modern Gardening'.

The placement of the essay was deliberate, and logical. Kent, said Walpole, had been 'a painter, an architect, and the father of modern gardening. In the first character, he was below mediocrity; in the second, he was a restorer of the science; in the last, an original, and the inventor of an art that realizes painting, and improves nature. Mahomet imagined an Elysium, but Kent created many.' In other words, Kent was a lousy artist ('His celebrated monument of Shakespeare in the Abbey was preposterous') but a brilliant landscape designer.

Walpole plainly regarded Kent as a handy peg on which to hang his own theories about gardening. 'On Modern Gardening' (actually written in 1770) fell precisely at a gardening watershed, and Walpole wrote with full consciousness of this fact. Gardening was hugely fashionable in the eighteenth century. (Perhaps 'garden making' would be more accurate, since the focus was less on horticulture than on design, usually on a scale involving many acres or whole countrysides.) There may be no era in history during which so much serious intellectual attention was given to the art, partly because there was enough money washing around the upper echelons of English society to encourage the embellishment of great rural estates, and partly because the best writers of the age, including Pope, were enchanted by the subject.

Walpole himself was a gardener, though 'gardenist', to use a contemporary term, might be more accurate (he never touched a spade). The frail, epicene, witty and comfortably wealthy son of Sir Robert Walpole, George II's powerful and corrupt prime minister, Walpole was in effect a professional dilettante and tastemaker. Strawberry Hill, his 'gothick' castle on the edge of London next to Pope's Thames-side villa, became a prime tourist attraction and cultural influence in spite of the fact that it was thoroughly bogus, constructed largely of lath and plaster made to look like stone. Predictably, Walpole had some strong opinions about gardening.

His main opinion, set forth in 'On Modern Gardening', was that the English – and, in particular, William Kent – had finally gotten it right. Since ancient times, designers had been on a completely wrong tack, creating trivial and contrived gardens, gardens that were 'anything but rural and verdant'. Even Pliny's Roman garden (conventionally regarded as admirable because classical) was, in Walpole's eyes, an abomination of 'boxtrees cut into monsters, animals, letters, and the names of the master and the artificer'. (Walpole was particularly offended by topiary.) Nor were medieval gardens any better, in his estimation – square, walled-off kitchen gardens, 'built to the exclusion of nature and prospect'. The magnificent formal expanses of seventeenth-century France, the avenues of trees, the intricate ground-embroidery of *parterre* – all these Walpole dismissed as 'impotent displays of false taste'. Why, in the garden of Marshal de Biron, he reports with repugnance, he saw 9,000 pots of asters lining the walks!

But now, thanks to such brilliant landscape architects as Kent (and indirectly to the poet John Milton, who had cosily characterized the Garden of Eden as 'a happy rural seat of various view'), the dismal mould of symmetry and stiffness was broken. As Walpole put it, 'absurdity could go no farther and the tide turned'. Nature would no longer be tormented, but respected. 'The garden was to be set free . . . from its prim regularity that it might assort with the wilder country without.'

The symbol Walpole chose to represent this liberation was appropriate: the ha-ha. In essence a sunken wall – you dig a ditch and build a wall along one face of it, *below* ground level – a ha-ha made it possible to join the lawn invisibly to the countryside, and still keep the cows out of the shrubberies. I suspect that this 'capital stroke, the leading step to all that followed' may have received its odd name when somebody fell into one; Walpole's less dramatic explanation is that the structures were 'so astonishing, that the common people called them Ha! Has! to express their surprise at finding a sudden and unperceived check to their walk'. In fact, the invention was probably French. But, whatever its derivation, Walpole regarded Kent as its hero. In his marvelous phrase, Kent 'leaped the fence and saw that all nature was a garden'.

There is no doubt that Walpole was on the mark here in spotting a seismic shift in gardening taste. The belief, as he put it, that the living landscape 'should be chastened or polished, not transformed' is one that is still with us. It guided the grandest manipulators of terrain, woods and water in Walpole's day and after; it inspired William Robinson and Gertrude Jekyll; and it continues to make sense to most of today's finest gardeners. Whether William Kent was its best exemplar, however, is open to question. He may have leaped the fence, but he found some pretty weird things on the other side.

Walpole pointed out a few of them. Kent got so carried away with imitating nature, he noted, that he planted dead trees in Kensington Gardens 'to give a greater air of truth to the scene'. (They didn't last – 'he was soon laughed out of this excess.') Kent firmly believed that nature abhorred a straight line, so he and his less talented successors made everything crooked. His plantings were 'puny' and aimed for too quick effect. And he was as guilty as anyone of the sin Walpole identified as being most threatening to the excellence of 'the modern style of gardening'. This was 'the pursuit of variety', the desperate search for the new and the exciting, for 'the gigantic, the puerile, the quaint . . . the barbarous, and the monkish'.

The trouble was that the eighteenth century was avid for novelties. In Kent's case, this lapse was best typified by the artificial hermitage, complete with real hermit. (I'm reminded of Marianne Moore's delightful description of a poem as 'an imaginary garden with a real toad in it'.) While it wouldn't be fair to blame him for inventing this particular bit of garden nuttiness,

the fact remains that he was responsible for designing and building what may be the most famous hermitage of all – Queen
Caroline's in Richmond Park.

Two buildings were involved, neither of which still exists.
The first, the Hermitage, was a neoclassical edifice constructed
in 1731 of somewhat battered stone sunk into the side of a hill.
The other, finished in 1735, was an especially bizarre affair called
Merlin's Cave. This 'indigested pile' (in the words of a contemporary magazine) boasted a thatched 'druidical' roof, an interior
assembled from tree trunks and branches, a library of edifying
books, and life-sized wax figures of a number of notables, including Queen Elizabeth I, Merlin and Merlin's secretary. Queen
Caroline's hired hermit was one Stephen Duck, a farm labourer
and self-taught poet, whose later career as rector of Byfleet and
governor of Duck Island in St James's Park came to a tragic
end when he drowned himself in the Thames. Just how long
he spent in the Queen's employ, letting his beard and fingernails grow (*de rigueur* for professional hermits) and disdaining
the company of men (apart from the floods of visitors), is un-
recorded. But presumably Duck was more successful than his
fellow hermit at Painshill in Surrey, who within three weeks
of signing a seven-year contract at £700 was caught sneaking
out to the pub. (It wasn't easy to get a good hermit; more than
one gentleman was reduced to staffing his hermitage with a
stuffed specimen.)

Walpole took a dim view of hermitages. 'It is almost comic,'
he wrote, 'to set aside a quarter of one's garden to be melancholy in.' Advisedly, he does not mention Kent's efforts in this
line in 'On Modern Gardening', though elsewhere he dismisses
the waxworks as 'this unintelligible puppetshow' and calls the
Hermitage 'another injudicious and ostentatious whim' of
Queen Caroline. He had little time for the Queen (who, he said,

'made great pretensions to learning and taste without much of the former and none of the latter'), so quite possibly he would have laid all the blame on her instead of Kent. After all, even Caroline's husband George II didn't have a lot of sympathy for her gardening efforts. 'You *deserve* to be abused,' he snorted, 'for such childish, silly stuff.'

In any case, Kent was never a pure exponent of the natural style. In his study of Kent's work, the historian John Dixon Hunt points out that the designer's taste was formed during his youthful years as an apprentice artist in Italy, and that he was exceedingly fond of classical bric-à-brac, from temples to statuary to triumphal gates and obelisks, and of Italianate formality. While he eventually did employ ha-has, and 'serpentined' his lakes and pathways, it wasn't until Lancelot 'Capability' Brown was in full flow a generation later that the free, romantic mode in landscape design really took over. Brown not only accepted Walpole's view that 'an open country is but a canvas on which a landscape might be designed', he was also fearlessly prepared to design it. As Cowper put it:

> He speaks. The lake in front becomes a lawn,
> Woods vanish, hills subside, and vallies rise:
> And streams, as if created for his use,
> Pursue the track of his directing wand.

Without making too much of it, I should note that it was Brown who, in the course of redesigning Richmond Park around 1770, demolished Merlin's Cave and 'Transform'd to lawn what once was Fairy land'.

Not surprisingly, after 250 years most of Kent's creations have gone the way of Merlin's Cave. The only full-scale garden left is Rousham in Oxfordshire, which is open to the public. Walpole regarded it as 'the most engaging of all Kent's works'. I happened to go there a couple of years ago on an overcast day in autumn, and, to tell the truth, the experience was a perfect illustration of the difficulty in doing justice to an ancient example of the landscape designer's art. Lacking the abundant cheap labour of the eighteenth century, the lawns looked scruffy and the trees unkempt; the little temples in the woods evoked public conveniences as much as Palladian Italy. Without a solid classical education it was impossible to grasp all the resonances of the Praeneste Terrace, copied from a famous Roman ruin, or, in the midst of a light drizzle, to appreciate the subtle iconography of the statues. Yet Rousham was beautiful, and a sense of this contained, intelligent, *designed* beauty stays with you, as it must have stayed with Horace Walpole, who found 'the whole, sweet'.

The Age of Hedges

A few years ago an English botanist named Max Hooper had a brilliant idea. It had to do with hedges. Hooper was studying the effects of insecticides on hedgerow plants when he noticed that English hedges varied a lot. Some were composed of no more than a single species, usually hawthorn, and these tended to run in straight lines. Other hedges, especially the wandering kind beloved of landscape artists and the English generally, boasted an impressive range of shrubs and trees, from hazels to oaks to several kinds of rose. Some, in fact, contained upwards of a dozen different species in a short stretch. Obviously the variation meant something. But what?

Hedges are ubiquitous in Britain. Estimates of just how many there are vary widely, but the best guess is somewhere between a third and a half million miles. You see them everywhere, especially in the south-west, and also along the Welsh and Scottish borders, wherever the land is not too high or rough. Not every farmer loves a hedge – starting in the Napoleonic era, when high grain prices encouraged bigger fields, a gradual process of grubbing out hedges has been going on, particularly in East Anglia and the east Midlands. Inconsistent government policy encouraged this until very recently (at one point a few years ago you could get a grant for demolishing a hedge, and at the same time could get a grant for planting one!). Even so, plenty remain. Some regions have so many roadside hedges that it is hard to see the scenery, and around our house on the edge of Wales the hills are absolutely patchworked with them. They are substantial hedges, too, made to hold Welsh mountain sheep, and they do. If you want to get through one, take an axe and figure on an afternoon.

To a naturalist, a hedgerow offers many delights. It is a shelter for birds and such little mammals as rabbits, shrews and (obviously) hedgehogs, and a habitat – sometimes the only really comfortable habitat left – for dozens of plant species from cowslips to cow-parsley. Hooper, however, viewed his hedges with different eyes. Soil types failed to explain the variations in the numbers of tree and shrub species in particular hedges. Neither, in most cases, did the climate. Could it be, he wondered, that the variations reflected the *age* of the hedges? After all, growing things change over time. Was it possible that we had here a sort of gigantic botanical clock?

To find out, he tracked down a selection of 227 hedges that could be dated with some accuracy from documentary evidence: old deeds, charters (some going back to Saxon times), the Domesday Book of 1086, monastic records, old maps. The hedges were scattered across England, from Devon in the south through Gloucestershire to Cambridgeshire, Huntingdonshire and Lincolnshire in the Midlands. Then (with some help) Hooper started counting species in randomly chosen 30-yard sections of each hedge. Arbitrarily excluded were blackberries (find a hedge without blackberries!) and woody climbers like ivy (ditto), but those counted included about fifty other common shrubs and trees from hedgerow hawthorn (*Crataegus monogyna*) to euonymus (*Euonymus europaeus*, known around here as spindle). The results were fascinating.

Within a surprisingly narrow range, Hooper found that the number of species in 30 yards of a given hedge correlated with the age of the hedge in centuries. A hedge known to have existed 1,000 years ago had at least ten species in it, an 800-year-old hedge eight species, a 100-year-old hedge just one. The margin of error could be as much as one or two centuries, but more often than not the numbers jibed. There was something satisfying, and at the same time slightly unearthly, about the idea that hedges aged this way. Nicest of all, of course, was the fact that anybody with a shrub and tree guide could go out, pace off 30 yards, count species and tell how old a particular hedge was.

Once Hooper's Rule received some publicity, plenty of people did this, among them several thousand schoolchildren enlisted by their science teachers to survey hedges all over the country. As the data came in, one fact about British hedges emerged with splendid clarity: there is an amazing number of *very* old hedges, hedges older by far than the oldest stag-headed oak squatting in a deer park, hedges to shame the antiquity of Tolkien's most elderly ent.

Previously, most historians of the countryside had assumed that the great majority of British hedges dated only from the time of parliamentary enclosures, when powerful landlords managed to get bills passed permitting them to enclose – and take over – open fields traditionally farmed and grazed in common by ordinary people. The planting of new hedges created pastures where cows and sheep could be left without herdsmen, thus further enriching the wealthy (and, incidentally, driving off a considerable number of impoverished farmers to urban slums or to America). Enclosures got started in the 1600s, reached a peak late in that century, and continued until the middle of the nineteenth century, when there wasn't much left to enclose. So if, in fact, most hedges were originally enclosure hedges, then most hedges ought to be 200 or 300 years old, at the outside.

We now know, thanks to Hooper's Rule, that fewer than half of Britain's hedges are the result of parliamentary enclosures, and most of these are in the east Midlands. Elsewhere, there are miles and miles of vastly older hedges still leafing out every spring. A quarter of the hedges in Devon are more than 800 years old, another quarter more than 700. In certain parts of Devon and Suffolk, researchers found that 80 per cent of the hedges contained between six and ten species, suggesting that they were between 600 and 1,000 years old. (Some, apparently, went back even farther than that, though no one seems prepared to pinpoint a Roman hedge using Hooper's Rule.)

In the course of all this counting, some other pleasant intricacies turned up. A close examination of the tabulation revealed that in addition to the *number* of species, the *type* of species growing in a hedge also said something about its age. For example, field maple (*Acer campestre*) generally did not appear until a hedge already contained four other species. Spindle, obviously a reluctant colonizer, came along only after there were six other species on hand. This meant that a hedge containing spindle could be judged to be at least 700 years old.

Is all this too good to be true? Why on earth should a rule as simple (or simple-minded) as this really work? I must say, it gives me a distinctly odd feeling to think of botanical life progressing on such an orderly timetable, passing like us through the generations, suffering its own crises and plagues and invasions, creating its own history. Hedges may indeed be planted by humans, but in this business they are showing an unsettling degree of independence.

Oliver Rackham, in his wonderful book *The History of the Countryside*, investigates why Hooper's Rule works and mentions a few exceptions – some of them rather arcane – that ought to be kept in mind while using it. The main reason it works, he notes, is that a hedge acquires species as it ages – but not readily. Seeds blow in; birds carry them in. A second reason is that hedges were planted with more species in earlier times than later. By parliamentary-enclosure days, professional nurserymen supplied huge quantities of seedlings, normally all of one kind. (This trade was the foundation of some of today's most prosperous British nursery firms.) Third, the older a hedge is, the more likely that it was converted from something else – the wild edge of a wood, or a collection of bushes left when the field was first cleared for cultivation.

These reasons why the rule works also suggest why in some cases it may not. For one thing, the terrain and climate in many regions are too harsh to allow the growth of all but a few species. For another, relatively modern enclosure-era hedges sometimes incorporated whatever suitable plants could be dug up in the wild, or were deliberately planted with a variety of species. English elm, a common hedgerow tree, can be a vigorous suckerer, squeezing out just about every other species (except blackberries) from old hedges that would otherwise have many. Then there is the Texas Exception. Rackham points out how barbed-wire fences put up on the prairies near Waco in the 1880s have gradually accumulated seedlings of Texas elm, black oak, Texas ash, prairie sumac, poison ivy and heaven knows what else, turning gradually into authentic hedges. The same thing can happen to a neglected English fence.

Still, handled with care, Hooper's Rule does offer a handy historical yardstick. I, for one, want to believe in it; I've lived here long enough to become thoroughly infected by the British love for local history. I delight in the notion that some Saxon shepherd leaned on his crook in my meadow a thousand years ago, recognizing that he may, in fact, have been a latecomer like me – Bronze Age hillforts crown nearly every protuberance in the neighbourhood. The other day I went so far as to count the species in the hedge that runs between our property and our neighbour's blackcurrant fields, just to see how old it is.

This particular hedge follows the parish boundary between Skenfrith and St Maughans. That alone suggests that it's pretty old, because parish boundaries can be ancient – pre-Norman, even pre-Roman in some cases. When I bought the place, it didn't look like a hedge at all. Nobody had cut it for years, and it had turned into an impenetrable mass of half-grown trees and full-grown bushes. I 'laid' it myself, which is to say that I cleaned it out, sawed down the unmanageable stuff and bent the remaining saplings and small trunks over at a 45-degree angle, chopping halfway through them with an axe when necessary to make them stay in place. That was four or five years ago. Now, with regular clippings, it looks like a normal hedge again.

I'm still not sure I did it right, but my species count in the 30-yard sample was nine, possibly ten. I found ash, probably two kinds of oak (*Quercus robur* and *Q. petraea*), hazel, elder, wild privet (*Ligustrum vulgare*), blackthorn, holly, hawthorn – and a spindle tree!

The spindle was the prize, of course. It means that my hedge is at least 700 years old, even if I made some mistakes. There is always the possibility that it was planted in 1977 by Mr Morris, the previous owner of Towerhill Cottage, but at the moment I regard this possibility as remote. I'm not inclined to investigate.

Walking Trees

There has always been something appealing about the idea of an instant garden. You start with nothing, except maybe an expanse of subsoil or, in grander cases, a couple of meadows and some sheep. Then *presto*! You've got a pleasure ground to be proud of, presumably low-maintenance and seasonally calculated for year-round appeal. No waiting for trees and shrubs to mature, no fiddle with half-bare borders, no little seedlings damping off in despair. All you need to do is hire a landscape designer, open your wallet and sit back.

The other day *The Times* had a sobering article about Mr and Mrs John Hoban, of Ormskirk, Lancashire. The Hobans, it seems, hired a landscape architect named Douglas Knight to transform their 1-acre plot into a spectacular 'water and rock garden' featuring a waterfall, a pond, three streams and an ornamental bridge. They paid him £25,000, which is spectacular enough in itself, but what they got was what Mrs Hoban described later – in court – as 'a cross between a paddy field and a moat'. The garden flooded every time it rained, requiring the Hobans to use emergency pumps. They even had to arrange for neighbours to be 'pond sitters', whenever they went away on holiday, in case of deluge.

The problem in this case was probably a simple matter of bad drains (not that *any* drainage problem is ever simple), but in a way it is typical of instant gardens. They are more prone than most gardens to engineering disasters. Or perhaps, to be nice about it, one might better say that they demand more of a designer's engineering skills.

Certainly this was true in the days when men like William Kent, Lancelot 'Capability' Brown and Humphry Repton were hard at work creating the ducal spreads that still dot the English countryside. Though they hardly look it now, those placid shapely lakes, those long sweeping lawns, mowed or nibbled, above all those trees – the ancient oaks and beeches, the rook-haunted groves of ash, the huge, ragged cedars of Lebanon – were the instant gardens of their time. Just as Mr and Mrs Hoban wanted quick results for their twenty-five grand, no self-respecting eighteenth-century gentleman in a mood for a new park was prepared to sit around for a decade or two waiting for his saplings to fill out.

A great deal has been written about the theory and aesthetics of landscape architecture's golden age, but curiously little about how the work was done. You have to look between the lines and consider, for example, what was involved in creating two broad lakes at Blenheim out of a trickle that (as Lord Berkeley disdainfully observed) 'you could, without straining, jump over'. Or how the designers brought their copses and clumps of trees into fully grown existence, in exactly the right places, within months rather than years.

The earthworks often were, by any standards, titanic. In his biography of 'Capability' Brown, Thomas Hinde points out that an estimated 23,500 cubic yards of earth had to be moved – all by hand, of course – to make the Grecian Valley at Stowe in 1746. The scene would have looked more like a battlefield than a garden, especially because the work went on in the depths of winter. In that season villagers could be hired for 8 pence a day instead of the usual 10, since there was no fieldwork available to compete for their labour. Also, the noble lord and his family would naturally be away in London for the season, and could thus be spared the pain of viewing such disorder.

So, provided there was money on hand to pay (not always the case), labour in quantity took the place of machinery. In one modest project at Sandleford Priory in 1782, twenty poor weavers from Newbury, 'who by the decay of our manufacture are devoid of employment', worked under the direction of an ex-boxer and reformed alcoholic. According to Elizabeth Montague, the wealthy widow whose grounds were being transformed, the weavers 'were not dextrous at the rake and pitchfork, but the plain digging and driving wheelbarrows they can perform and are very glad to get their daily subsistence'. All went swimmingly until the foreman became a religious fanatic, went mad, and tried to atone for his past transgressions by eating grass.

As a rule, though, the technical aspects of landscape manipulation gave more trouble than the labour. Calculating water levels and exact land contours required sophisticated surveys using equipment primitive by modern standards. Hydraulic engineering was in its infancy. Constructing a lake for the Second Earl of Egremont at Petworth, Brown was forced not only to move a 'vast deal' of earth, but also to build a complicated clay-cored dam with a brick-lined drainage tunnel at its base. As it happened, Egremont was a notoriously tetchy client (which might have been predicted from his famous comment, while serving as ambassador to the Congress of Augsburg in 1761, that if he survived his next three turtle dinners he would become immortal), and complained that his new lake wouldn't hold water. Eventually, it settled down, and did, and does.

Brown's aquatic operations at Harewood in Yorkshire were also fraught. There, he spent three years excavating a lake for the rich heir of a West Indian sugar fortune. In 1777 workmen finally ran the plug into the dam head and waited for the lake to fill. 'You will if possible be more surprised than I was,' the unsettled Harewood steward wrote to his master, 'when I tell you that the water ran out half as fast as it came in.' Hurried patching to the clay wall ensued and the leak stopped. The lake is still there.

If water was one key element in the creation of great instant gardens of the era, planting was the other. There is a story, probably apocryphal, of Brown announcing to a gentleman with a more than normally dreary piece of property, 'My lord, there is nothing to be done here unless you plant one half of your estate and lay the other half under water.' 'Planting' meant planting trees. The aim was 'speedy effect', with romantic glades, avenues and walks that could be enjoyed without delay.

Such planting was done on an industrial scale, as can be determined from surviving nurserymen's bills and other documents. In each of six winters in the 1770s, for instance, Brown planted from a low of 36,000 to a high of 91,000 trees for Lord Weymouth at Longleat. One problem was protecting the new plantings from the depredations of cows and sheep. In his treatise *The Rural Improver*, the landscaper William Pontey plumped for the new wire fence as more fashionable than 'lumberly' wooden posts and rails. Sir Walter Scott, whose vast plantings at Abbotsford may have helped take his mind off his endless literary labours, struck on a more ingenious method: He inserted his new saplings into the middle of prickly gorse bushes.

The challenge was to move trees as large as possible. Such endeavours had a long, if chequered, history by that time. In 1670, the great French landscape architect le Nôtre was said to have moved most of the trees of the Bois de Boulogne from Versailles to the edge of Paris, employing what a contemporary German writer delightfully termed '*die grosse Gartenmaschine*'. Just what this consisted of isn't certain, but the reference is probably to a monstrous four-wheeled iron contraption reportedly stored at Versailles until the French Revolution, when it was 'converted to pikes'. In the mid-seventeenth century, the antiquarian and tree lover John Evelyn had proposed a method of trenching a tree, propping the earth around it with blocks and then, when the weather dropped below freezing, pouring in water. In theory, one could then move the tree with its soil and roots intact. Exactly how such a move was to be accomplished, given the weight, remains unexplained.

Brown's stroke of genius was to recognize that a tree did not have to be moved standing upright. He (or perhaps one of his workmen) devised a Transplanting Machine consisting of a long, thick pole fastened at one end to an axle fitted with two strong cartwheels. The pole, held vertically, was strapped to the tree trunk. Ropes drawn by a number of husky men – or a horse – gradually pulled the top of the pole downward to horizontal, the tree with it, wrenching the entire mass of roots out of the ground. A team of horses or oxen could then trundle the tree, roots first, off to its new planting place in a 'clump', 'grove' or 'skreen'. Brown typically transplanted trees up to 36 feet high in this effective, if slightly brutal, way.

Judging from the comments of subsequent planters, many of Brown's transplants must have suffered. One writer spoke derisively of his 'vigorous and short-hand method of tearing trees up by the roots'. Pontey, writing in 1828, is sceptical about the practice of moving full-grown trees, 'as the business is extremely tedious, and hazardous also; and after all, in cases of success, such trees for several years grow so slowly as to remind one of the stricken deer'. It was expensive, too, as another commentator noted: 'Three men moving plants, near *twenty* feet high, and as thick as the leg . . . do not move more than six or eight plants a day.' Still, nobody was prepared to admit that it couldn't, or shouldn't, be done.

Brown apparently did not hesitate to lop branches and roots in order to lighten the load when moving a tree; in fact he sometimes 'quite pollarded' it. William Marshall, the respected author of *Planting and Rural Ornament* (1796), was not much kinder. Though he scrupulously refused to prune any roots, he believed that 'forest trees, and other stem plants, may in general be trimmed closely' because this left roots with less top-growth to feed. 'The most rational, the most *natural*, and, at the same time, the most elegant, manner of doing this is to prune the boughs, in such a manner as to form the head of the plant into a conoid, in resemblance of the natural head of the Lombardy poplar.'

Not every gentleman, however, cared to have the beeches in his grove looking like giant Belgian endives. One who objected, and did something about it, was Sir Henry Steuart, Baronet, a minor Scottish lord whose estate of Allanton lay in what are now the dingy industrial outskirts of Glasgow. He devoted his life to transplanting trees and wrote a book about his techniques that was published and republished in both Britain and the United States. Sir Walter Scott found him 'a most fantastic person . . . a solemn prosing serious fop'. But even he had to admit that Steuart 'exercises wonderful power over the vegetable world, and has made his trees dance about as merrily as did Orpheus'.

Sir Henry's boast was that 'an *entire park* could be wooded at once, and forty years of life anticipated'. Moreover, it could be done without 'lopping or mutilating the Trees'. The secret of what he called 'the art of giving immediate effect to wood' was actually not very secret. It consisted mostly of taking great care in (1) selecting the best tree to move (no taller than 36 feet, or shorter than 15); (2) preparing the ground for planting (digging deeply and widely, using plenty of manure); (3) getting the tree ready (this might mean putting down a sloping layer of soil, peat and cinders to encourage the roots to grow closer to the surface, or trenching around the tree, introducing good soil and peat and waiting up to six years for a more compact root ball to form); and (4) meticulously uncovering the entire root structure, root by fine root, using a special hand pick for the purpose. When it came time to move the tree, Steuart advised using a refined version of 'Capability''s old pole and wheels, sometimes with a third wheel in the rear, but not until freeing the whole tree save for a 6- or 8-foot ball of earth and turf in the root ball's centre. Replanting was to take place immediately – within a week at most, unless there was a sudden freeze – with the tree's orientation reversed, so that the former south side faced north. No trampling the infill, either – soil was to be spread carefully over the roots a layer at a time, and then 'dashed down' with buckets of water.

Significantly, Steuart had little to say about the need to keep roots from drying out, or to avoid disturbance, the sorts of consideration modern transplanters would place foremost. But many of his procedures do make sense, if for the wrong reasons. And they clearly worked. Certain trees, he noted, were easier to transplant than others. Easiest of all was ash, no surprise to anyone who has made beanpoles out of green ash sticks and seen them sprout as fast as the beans. The most difficult was oak. Horse chestnut could be moved in just about any season, and you could hardly miss with an elm, at least not a Scotch elm. Beech, he admitted, was 'dorty' – a Scots word meaning something like 'capricious' or 'wayward'. But most of his trees danced merrily.

So, on one occasion, did a couple of his workmen as they were moving a large tree. Steuart tells the story:

In proceeding with the machine down a gentle slope of some length, at an accelerated pace, on which occasion both the balancemen had gained the top with their usual agility, it so fell out that the cords which secured the rackpins of the root unfortunately gave way. This happened so suddenly that the root at once struck the ground, with a force equal to the united weight of the mass and the momentum of the movement, and pitched the balancemen (now suddenly lifted to an elevation of nearly thirty feet), like two shuttlecocks, to many yards distance, over the heads of the horses and the driver, who stood in amazement at their sudden and aerial flight! Luckily for the men, there was no frost upon the ground, so that, instead of breaking their bones, they fell only on the soft turf of the park, from which soon getting up, and shaking themselves, they heartily joined in the laughter of their companions at the leap which they had taken.

Inexperienced planters were warned to take note. The balancemen, for their part, didn't need a warning: 'It proved impossible,' Steuart remarked, 'to persuade them to resume their elevated functions for many months after.'

Nowadays, landscape architects can get along without balancemen; they have cranes and earth-moving equipment to assist them, to say nothing of plumbers. But there is no lack of demand for instant gardens, albeit on a smaller scale. As a postscript to the Hoban Affair, it is worth noting that our latter-day 'Capability' Brown, Douglas Knight, won another medal at the Chelsea Flower Show last spring for a truly impressive artificial hillside containing dozens of huge rocks, two or three waterfalls, various grasses, rock plants, shrubs and possibly trout. No big trees, though. This creation went to a private buyer within minutes on opening day, for the familiar £25,000.

Forsyth's Plaister

It would be pleasant to have a plant named after you. The nearest I can come to this honour is a plant named *Elliottia*, which I ran across in *The Plant Finder* and for which I can claim no credit whatsoever. I didn't discover it, name it or grow it; in fact I don't even know what it looks like, except that, according to the book, it is a member of the Ericaceae family. Only two cultivars are listed, and one of those has been deleted, presumably for lack of interest. A single nursery stocks the other. Not an impressive show for *Elliottia*.

By contrast, the name of William Forsyth will always be green or, rather, yellow. Who does not know *Forsythia*? Oddly enough, however, though it *was* named after him, he had as little to do with *Forsythia* as I did with *Elliottia*. What we – I, anyway – remember him for is something else entirely: one of the more engaging episodes of chicanery in the history of horticulture. A good hoax is hard to resist, even one that, at this distance, is impossible to pin down as deliberate.

William Forsyth was a distinguished figure in eighteenth-century horticulture. Born in Aberdeenshire in 1737, he made his way south and first turns up working as a gardener for the Duke of Northumberland at Syon House, near London. In 1770, having by that time made a name for himself, he was appointed to the plum job of chief gardener of the Apothecaries' Garden in Chelsea, the still surviving enclave better known as the Chelsea Physic Garden.

There Forsyth immediately got to work on two projects. One was to build a rock garden – probably one of the first to be deliberately constructed – out of 40 tons of stone from the Tower of London, some chunks of flint and chalk and a large quantity of volcanic rock brought back from Iceland by the explorer Joseph Banks. The other project – more significant in view of Forsyth's later ventures – was to cut down a number of trees growing in the garden, either because they were badly decayed or because their shade interfered with the growth of medicinal plants.

Except for complaining about his salary (at one point he was given permission to sell surplus plants in order to make ends meet), Forsyth seems to have stuck quietly to his trowel. In 1784, however, he was invited to move up a notch, becoming the king's gardener at Kensington Gardens and St James's Gardens, in the heart of London. This meant a new field of specialization, since one of the main functions of Kensington Gardens was to furnish the royal table with fruit and vegetables.

A problem immediately presented itself. Many of the old fruit trees were in bad shape, overgrown and diseased, leaking gum from wounds; there were cankers on the apple trees. Forsyth didn't dare interrupt the royal fruit supply by replanting everything, so he set to work restoring the old trees to health. He lopped heads, cut off over-large and dead branches and generally cleaned up. And in the course of doing so he developed his great invention: a miraculous 'plaister' that not only sealed wounds in bark, protected stumps left by pruning and prevented further decay, but actually (so Forsyth was to claim) cured old, damaged and rotting trees of whatever ailed them, making them as good as new!

Needless to say, people talked about Forsyth's plaister. He was by then a prominent figure in horticultural circles – a founding member of a precursor of the Royal Horticultural Society; a correspondent of many famous and titled gardeners, from the Earl of Buchan to the president of the Board of Agriculture; and an assiduous collector of plants, mosses, seaweeds, rocks and fossils from many corners of the globe. In 1789 he received a letter from two high officials of the Land Revenue Office. 'Being informed that you have discovered a method of curing defects in growing trees of all ages, which may have sustained damage from any cause whatever,' the letter began, 'we wish to be favoured by you with an answer to the following questions.' The letter went on to ask Forsyth pointedly what he knew about damage to oak trees and a possible cure for defects in growing timber, including a query about exactly how much it might cost 'to apply such a remedy to a very considerable number of trees'.

The background of the inquiry was obvious enough. In 1789 Britain was thoroughly shaken by events in revolutionary France, and the navy, which was the bulwark of Britain's defences, was as dependent on oak as it would be on steel today.

Forsyth's response to the letter was quick and positive. He was in a position to assure the gentlemen that while damage to the bark of an oak tree could, if untreated, ruin the timber, if not actually kill the tree, they need not despair. His treatment (which was, incidentally, 'known only to myself') could render damaged trees 'as fit for the navy, as though they had never been injured'. This had been demonstrated by 'a great variety of experiments on fruit and forest trees, in His Majesty's gardens at Kensington . . . To heal any wounded tree, and even to restore it to its former health, if there be only an inch or two of bark

remaining to carry on the circulation of the vegetable œconomy';
all that was necessary was to cut out the decay and apply the
plaister. While he was rather tied up with the royal gardens, he
would be happy to send along some samples of healed wood, or
to show the gentlemen trees that had been cured. The cost of
the treatment would be of the order of sixpence a tree, leaving
the question of payment to the inventor 'wholly and altogether
to your further consideration'.

A few weeks later, on a Saturday afternoon, an august committee of noble lords and other members drawn from both houses
of Parliament assembled at Kensington Gardens, under orders to
'ascertain the efficacy of a remedy invented by William Forsyth'. If they could be convinced of its manifold virtues then
Forsyth was to receive suitable recompense for divulging his
secret.

Forsyth offered them documents and explained the composition of his plaister (it was a mixture of cow dung, lime rubbish
from old buildings – preferably 'cielings' – wood ash and sand).
He demonstrated how to use it (trim back the dead wood, then
lay on the plaister an eighth of an inch thick, powdering the
surface with wood and bone ash until dry). And he exhibited
trees that had been treated. The latter were impressive – at least
the committee was impressed. Most of the trees on display happened to be elms, horse chestnuts and limes (the only available
oaks had been treated too recently for complete recovery, Forsyth explained), but the results appeared highly satisfactory.
New trees were growing vigorously out of 'decayed and hollow
stumps', and the quality of the wood regrown in damaged places
was judged 'after as accurate a secreting and comparison as we
were able to make', to be indistinguishable from the original.

Possibly it *was* the original. In any case, I like to think of the
bewigged gentlemen strolling through the royal gardens on that

autumn afternoon, gazing at the trees and fingering bits of wood. It must have been sunny and pleasant. Certainly their report breathes uncritical amiability, concluding that 'we . . . do not hesitate to express our conviction, that Mr Forsyth's composition is a discovery which may be highly beneficial both to individuals and the public.' So little did they hesitate, in fact, that before long Forsyth had been presented with a royal grant of £1,500, worth about £90,000 in modern terms. The recipe for his plaister appeared in the London *Gazette* and many regional newspapers.

If at this stage Forsyth had kept his head down and restrained his friends, the whole matter might have passed quietly away at a cost of no more than a few frustrated silviculturists and unredeemed elm stumps. But, puffed with his success, he wrote and published – at his own expense – a little book bragging about the excellence of his invention and reprinting the committee's flattering report. This attracted some attention, and a long, laudatory article by a fellow Scot and old friend, James Anderson, the proprietor of a monthly journal called *Recreations in Agriculture*, attracted more. Forsyth's only failure, Anderson maintained, was to have been overly scrupulous. If, instead of accepting the government grant, he had promoted his discovery by some other means, he could have made much more money.

As a step in this direction, in 1802 Forsyth published a book entitled *A Treatise on the Culture and Management of Fruit Trees*, including a revised version of his tree-remedy pamphlet as a postscript. This time around, rumblings of discontent began to be heard in the higher reaches of the horticultural community. Critics noted that Forsyth had apparently borrowed most of his text from previous writers. Worse, suspicions about the value of the plaister were beginning to surface. The most outspoken sceptic was Thomas Andrew Knight, a 'distinguished cultivator' and pomologist from Herefordshire.

Forsyth's primary claim – that the plaister would rejuvenate hollow stumps and make damaged trees whole again, fit for naval use – struck Knight as nothing less than preposterous. The fact that Forsyth had received a grant of public money was an outrage. Why, the very idea of a lime and cow-dung wash was nothing new. The only new thing, Knight maintained, was Forsyth's extraordinary and quite unacceptable belief in its efficacy.

After a visit to Kensington Gardens to view Forsyth's trees, Knight commented that the 'composition' didn't appear to have done a lot for Forsyth's apples, and that he personally didn't put much stock in *any* 'topical application' to treat tree wounds or diseases. This remark infuriated Forsyth and his friend Anderson, who promptly devoted twelve and a half pages of *Recreations in Agriculture* to a defence of the plaister and an attack on Knight, accusing him in passing of 'misrepresentation'.

Knight came back with all guns firing. The hidden motive behind Anderson's attack, he suggested, was that Forsyth had been promised *another* £1,500 if his results could be duplicated, and any public doubts might imperil this payment. His own doubts were entirely clear. He had seen that new branches on a pear tree, claimed by Forsyth to have been stimulated into growth by application of the plaister five years before, were, in fact, only three years old, and probably would have grown anyway. As to the 'enormous crops of fruit' reportedly borne by the treated trees, he said, 'I cannot really speak, the plaistered trees having almost wholly failed to bear any in the only season I was in Mr Forsyth's garden.' But, he noted slyly, no doubt His Majesty's table was always abundantly supplied; the produce market at Covent Garden was within easy reach.

Knight published his strictures in a pamphlet in 1802. In 1803, in a second edition of his *Treatise*, Forsyth made a fairly weak rejoinder, without mentioning 'holes in trees'; a few months later, in yet another edition, he presented some support for himself in the form of a testimonial letter signed by a group of medical men, including a veterinary surgeon. The chief signatory was a Dr Lettsom, a gardening friend of Forsyth and a physician best remembered as the butt of a rhyme:

When any sick to me apply
I physicks, bleeds and sweats 'em,
If, after that, they choose to die,
Why, Verily! I. Lettsom.

The testimonial stated flatly that the doctors had examined Forsyth's trees and believed everything he had claimed for his discovery.

An annoyed Knight instantly wrote to Lettsom offering to bet him substantial amounts that he couldn't produce evidence in the form of actual timber samples that Forsyth's plaister worked. Lettsom, a Quaker, declined to take part in 'gaming', but eventually replied to Knight in the pages of *Gentleman's Magazine*, supplying two plates of tree sections that allegedly illustrated the plaister's marvellous curative powers. The plates were a mistake. Knight pounced, easily demonstrating that, far from supporting Forsyth, they, in fact, proved the opposite. One picture showed so many annual layers of wood around the cavity that, Knight said, 'Mr F's composition appears to have operated at least twelve years before it was ever applied!' while in the other there was no sign of new and old wood uniting, as the plaister was supposed to effect.

With that, the controversy petered out. Nothing more was heard from Anderson or Lettsom. Knight went on to other triumphs, in 1811 assuming the presidency of the new Royal Horticultural Society, a position he was to hold until his death in 1838. And William Forsyth, the king's gardener, was in no position to continue defending his plaister from among the pippins in Kensington, having died in 1804.

But if Forsyth's plaister was doomed to oblivion, Forsyth's name was not. It was a near thing, though. Back in 1788, when the great man's reputation was still unsullied, Thomas Walter published *Flora Caroliniana*, a survey of plants from the Carolinas. To one plant, a rather undistinguished climber, he gave the name *Forsythia*, in honour of William.

Walter, however, was not the best of botanists, and it subsequently developed that the climber already had a name – *Decumaria*. This turned out to be fortunate for Forsyth, because his name was then available to Martin Vahl, a Danish botanist, when he decided that a somewhat garish flowering shrub first reported from Japan in 1786 deserved to be in a genus of its own. Vahl dubbed it *Forsythia*, and *Forsythia* it is today. In 1844 the plant hunter Robert Fortune brought the first living specimens from the Orient to England, and its descendants are now blooming – quite unplaistered – in gardens all around the world.

The Great Water-lily

It has always been our endeavour to commence a New Year in this Magazine with some eminently rare or beautiful plant; but never had we the good fortune on any occasion to devote a Number to a production of such pre-eminent beauty, rarity, and we may add celebrity, as that now presented to our Subscribers ... Seldom has any plant excited such attention in the botanical world ...

The new year was 1847, and with these words the distinguished editor of *Curtis's Botanical Magazine* (and director of Kew), Sir William Hooker, began a fresh volume. His enthusiasm was understandable, if uncharacteristic. For the plant in question was indeed a marvel – the biggest water-lily anybody had ever laid eyes on, a spectacular monster described by one of the few Europeans to see it blooming in its native habitat as 'a vegetable wonder!' No more than a rumour for years, though a well-publicized one, the plant was now at last alive and growing in a warm pool at Kew, far from its South American home, and proudly bearing the name of the Queen herself – *Victoria regia*.

It was, as E. B. White's Charlotte might have said, some water-lily. Boasting leaves up to 6 feet in diameter, turned up at the edges to show their brilliant crimson undersides, it bore flowers as much as 15 inches across that gave off an extraordinary rich pineapple scent. Of course, Sir William admitted, the plants growing at Kew hadn't actually flowered yet ('Many are the disappointments and delays of Science!'), but there was reason for hope, and dried specimens were available to substantiate – at least in part – the accounts of gob-smacked travellers.

Victoria had been a long time arriving in England. In fact, it had been a long time emerging from the stagnant backwaters of the Amazon basin, where the German botanist Thaddäus Haenke, journeying through the region on a mission for the Spanish government, apparently first spotted it in about 1801. He had reportedly fallen on his knees 'in a transport of admiration' (a good trick, considering that he was travelling in a dugout canoe at the time). But if Haenke gathered specimens, they never reached Europe; all of his huge botanical collections vanished after his death in Bolivia in 1817.

Word, however, must have got round. About twenty years after Haenke's sighting Aimé Bonpland, a French botanist, explorer and colleague of the famous Alexander von Humboldt, discovered the *Victoria* growing in a river in the Bolivian province of Corrientes, near the Paraguayan border. He saw 'this superb plant' at a distance, and 'well nigh precipitated himself off the raft into the river in his desire to secure specimens'. Whether he got them or not is unclear; what is clear is that it was not until 1828 that another Frenchman, A. D'Orbigny, managed to send a collection of leaves, flowers and seeds, some dried and some pickled in spirits, to the Museum of Natural History in Paris. Like Bonpland, D'Orbigny found his water-lilies in Corrientes, and upon seeing them was 'struck with profound emotion'.

Unfortunately for D'Orbigny and the *gloire* of France, nobody in Paris got around to writing up and publishing his find. The specimens mouldered away unremarked, to the point where nothing remained but a single gigantic leaf, 'of immense dimensions and somewhat injured', Hooker reported, 'which had been folded for insertion into the Herbarium'. At this point, the French having blown it, the British stepped in.

Robert Schomburgk was, despite his name, at least an honorary Englishman. (He would eventually be knighted and serve as a British diplomat.) While still in his twenties, he had left his native Germany to follow his interest in geography and natural history in the Caribbean and South America, choosing British territories to explore (there were plenty), and developing such a reputation that in 1831 the Royal Geographical Society commissioned him to make a survey of British Guiana. It was in the course of this investigation that, proceeding up the River Berbice 'while contending with the difficulties that nature interposed in different forms', Schomburgk found a bay full of giant water-lilies. 'All calamities were forgotten; I was a botanist, and felt myself rewarded!' Unlike his predecessors, he succeeded not only in collecting a variety of specimens – leaves, flowers and fruit – but in getting them back to London. They were, it must be said, in a rather mangled and smelly state, yet not too far gone to be formally described by the botanist John Lindley, who published news of the discovery and firmly identified it as a new genus. This gave him the right to name it (much to French discomfiture), and he naturally chose to celebrate the newly crowned young queen.

Now the challenge was explicit: who would be the first in Britain – and it simply had to be Britain – to grow a live *Victoria* and watch it bloom? In 1845 the traveller Thomas Bridges, out shooting one afternoon in the interior of Bolivia, came across a pond filled with water-lilies and alligators. Caution prevailed; he recruited some Indians and a canoe before attempting to collect specimens of flowers, leaves and seeds. Even so, it was a tricky business; the 'tottering little bark' had room for only two of the huge leaves per trip, and when enough had been collected, he had to convince the doubtful Indians to haul the obviously useless load on carrying poles back to the village.

Bridges dried the leaves, preserved the flowers in spirits and packed the seeds in wet clay, then thought to be the best way to keep them alive during the journey to England. *En route*, predictably, most of them went bad. But out of the twenty-two seeds that Kew eagerly bought from him on arrival, two did germinate, calling forth Sir William's New Year effusion. The great water-lily was alive and growing. The question was whether or not it would ever bloom before dying.

As the years passed, prospects became dimmer. The plants remained alive at Kew, but showed no signs of blooming. At this point, in the summer of 1849, a great gardener took over. Joseph Paxton – later Sir Joseph, and the genius behind the Crystal Palace – had been superintendent of the Duke of Devonshire's magnificent gardens at Chatsworth for many years. If anyone knew how to make a *Victoria* flower, it was Paxton; this was a man who had produced bananas for the ducal table as early as 1842. Chatsworth's famous 'Great Stove' – a magnificent glass conservatory, the world's largest – had been built under his auspices. After constructing a special heated tank 12 feet square and 3 feet deep inside the conservatory, with a small waterwheel to keep the water moving gently, Paxton prevailed on Hooker to let him have one of the precious plants. He personally whisked it off to Chatsworth by fast train early one morning.

As the drama began, the Duke was away at Lismore in Ireland, but Paxton kept him posted. The *Victoria* planted in the new tank was tiny. Of its five leaves, the largest was less than 6 inches across. But it was clearly happier than at Kew, because within a month the large leaf measured 3½ *feet*, and was still growing. In another month it had hit 4½ feet, and the tank was getting distinctly crowded. Then, on 2 November, Paxton sent a triumphant message to Ireland: 'Victoria has shown flower!! An enormous bud like a poppy head made its appearance yesterday. It looks like a large peach placed in a cup. No words can describe the grandeur and beauty of the plant.'

And with that the water-lily craze really took off. The Duke hurried back from Ireland to witness the short-lived bloom – the first bud opened on 9 November, at night, and within thirty-six hours had decayed and sunk. Hooker came north, speeded by Paxton's assurance that 'The sight is worth a journey of a thousand miles.' Paxton presented Queen Victoria with a leaf and a flower bud. Dozens of curiosity-seekers, titled and otherwise, turned up to gape, especially at the gigantic leaves, which were supposed to be able to support the weight of a human. In high spirits, the Duke and Paxton dressed Paxton's seven-year-old daughter Annie as a fairy and stood her on one of the huge green saucers, inspiring the journalist Douglas Jerrold to a burst of Victorian sentimentality:

> On unbent leaf in fairy guise,
> Reflected in the water,
> Beloved, admired by hearts and eyes,
> Stands Annie, Paxton's daughter.
>
> Accept a wish, my little maid,
> Begotten at the minute,
> That scenes so bright may never fade –
> You still the fairy in it.
>
> That all your life nor care nor grief
> May load the wingéd hours
> With weight to bend a lily's leaf,
> But all around be flowers.

The image was unforgettable, so much so that perching a child on a *Victoria* leaf became a photographic cliché.

It suddenly seemed as though flowers were indeed 'all around'. Designers with an eye to the main chance quickly cobbled up lily-motif fireplaces, chandeliers and gas-jet holders (Queen Victoria herself bought a bronze three-light gas bracket decorated with lilies). One art historian notes that 'whole beds of water-lilies floated on Victorian floors, with the blue of the sky reflected enchantingly between the interstices of the lily-pads.' Vases, pitchers, cups and saucers, even an entire lily-shaped baby's cradle made of papier-mâché (the 'Victoria Regia Cot'), answered public demand. Leaves and blossoms appeared on fabrics and wallpapers in such profusion as to suggest that the twining stems, if not the roots, of Art Nouveau lay here.

In the meantime, as if enjoying all the attention, the Chatsworth *Victoria* thrived, producing in the course of a year no fewer than 140 leaves, 112 flower buds and many 'fine plump seeds'. To cultivate the new marvel properly, Paxton moved it from the Great Stove into a spacious new water-lily house, and before long Kew had a water-lily house too.

As it turned out, the lily was not all that hard to grow, provided the conditions were right. If they were *really* right (as in St Louis in 1896, where a leaf on a championship specimen proved capable of bearing a weight of 250 pounds), giant lilies could cover a pond in no time. Botanical explorers discovered other varieties in South America and breeders went to work to produce *Victoria* hybrids.

These days you can still see *V. regia* (now distinguished from others of the genus by the name *V. amazonica*) blooming in a lily house at Chatsworth. The Great Stove, regrettably, is gone, dynamited by the Ninth Duke in 1919 in a fit of frustration at the number of precious plants lost in World War I fuel shortages. At Kew, *Victoria* has been at home since 1987 in the new Princess of Wales Conservatory.

Yet today the fashion for enormous water-lilies whose leaves can support little girls seems to be fading, at least in Britain. Until about five years ago, in case you wanted something to startle the frogs in your pond, you could still buy a nursery-grown *V. amazonica*. Since then, according to that definitive manual *The Plant Finder*, they are no longer available. Perhaps it's just as well. Far from Victoria's fog-bound kingdom, the famous Brazilian landscape architect Roberto Burle Marx has found more appropriate ways to use them in gardens, with great elegance and nothing of the freak-show. I suspect that even Paxton might – after thinking about it – be prepared to step aside.

The Terrible Garden of
Sir William Chambers

It would be tedious to enumerate all the errors of false taste, but the havock it has made in our old plantations, must ever be remembered with indignation: the ax has often, in one day, laid waste the growth of several ages, and thousands of venerable plants, whole woods of them, have been swept away, to make room for a little grass, and a few American weeds.

Now, there speaks an angry man. His name was Sir William Chambers, and his diatribe, written in 1772, was aimed straight at the leading landscape designer of the day, the great Lancelot 'Capability' Brown. As the darling of every wealthy landowner with a country estate to spend money on, Brown had indeed swept away a lot of trees (and planted a lot of new ones). More to the point, he was famously the principal figure in the whole new, distinctively English fashion for a more natural landscape, for lakes and carefully placed groves and splendid long expanses of shaved lawn. In short, Brown was riding high. Provided the funds held out, he appeared set to 'improve' the entire face of England – not only the grand estates, which to some extent qualified for such treatment, but hundreds of more modest country seats that often didn't.

Enthusiasm for Brown's tactics was not, however, universal.

Some people rather missed the terraces and old-fashioned *parterres* he obliterated from around the houses (where did the garden go?). Horace Walpole deplored the way a house was often 'left grazing by itself in the middle of the park'. Still others – perhaps because they couldn't afford the gigantic earthworks – complained that there wasn't much point in paying to make the place look like countryside, when you could have countryside free. And as time went on and Brown's lakes and groves multiplied, another more basic rumble of discontent began to be heard. This kind of gardening – no flowers, nothing but trees, water and grass – was *boring*.

It was at that point that William Chambers, a prominent architect, delivered himself of *A Dissertation on Oriental Gardening*. At another time, perhaps, when landscape gardening as an art was less in the air, it might well have been dismissed as a bit of eccentric scholarship. Who, after all, knew or cared much about Chinese gardens, or China either, for that matter? What could they have to do with the spacious glories of the English countryside?

In fact, the notion of a Chinese garden – so exotic that almost nobody had any real idea what it was – had been haunting Europe for a long time. A hundred years before, in an influential essay called 'On the Gardens of Epicurus', Sir William Temple had praised them, contrasting European garden formality with the oriental love of irregularity, and claiming that the Chinese even had a particular word to express 'this Sort of Beauty': *Sharawadgi*.* He also recommended that European gardeners

---

*I hope I will not be regarded as showing off if I say that I happen to know some Chinese, and neither I nor generations of speculators since Temple's time have been able to figure out what Chinese word or phrase he could be referring to. Frankly, I think he made it up.

avoid trying to imitate their Eastern fellows: 'They are Adventures of too hard Achievement for any common hands.'

Whether or not Temple was right, pretty soon it didn't matter. The great day of 'Capability' Brown was dawning. English landscape architects like Charles Bridgeman, William Kent and, ultimately, Brown himself were establishing 'irregularity' on a basis that had nothing to do with Chinese ideas, declaring that 'all nature was a garden' and doing their expensive best to manipulate it. China itself remained at the back of people's minds as fascinating but somewhat unreal, a never-never-land of porcelains and bric-à-brac, of painted wallpapers, odd figures wearing big hats, half-moon bridges and delicate structures with bells on the turned-up eaves.

Yet if no one had much direct knowledge of China, that did not prevent its being hugely fashionable, a situation that William Chambers was able to turn to his advantage. He had, exceptionally, gained his acquaintance with Chinese things first-hand. As a young man, before becoming an architect, he made two voyages to Canton in the service of the Swedish East India Company, and had lived there for several months. In 1757, spotting a trend, he published *Designs of Chinese Buildings, Furniture, Dresses, Machines and Utensils* and for good measure threw in some of the principles of Chinese gardening he had learned, he said, from 'Lepqua, a celebrated Chinese painter'. As Chambers reported them, these notions were fairly unexceptionable, even in terms of what the English landscapists were then executing: 'Nature is their pattern, and their aim is to imitate her in all her beautiful irregularities.' The Chinese achieved this by applying a certain amount of conscious art to create a variety of pleasing scenes, which were then combined into 'an elegant and striking whole'.

But there were nevertheless hints in Chambers's account suggesting that admiring Chinese practice was not quite the same thing as admiring what the English landscape designers – particularly 'Capability' Brown – were doing. Rather than simply idealizing nature, the Chinese were prepared, according to Chambers, to elaborate it, making caves and grottoes, placing 'little temples, or other buildings' atop 'artificial rocks', devising surprises and amusements for the garden visitor. Brown, on the other hand, preferred elegance on the grand scale, with no fiddle.

Chambers – who was notably touchy – and Brown first came into direct contact at Kew, where Chambers, as a high-ranking royal architect (and, incidentally, a member of the Board of Works, to which Brown answered), was commissioned by Princess Augusta to design a number of decorative buildings in the area now covered by the Botanic Gardens. By 1763 he had put up no fewer than thirty temples and other structures, including the well-known (and still surviving) Chinese pagoda. Meanwhile, Brown was engaged to landscape the neighbouring grounds of Richmond Palace, and performed his usual job of large-scale destruction, clearing and replanting. At the same time as this dusty work was going on, Chambers was trying to construct a number of garden buildings around Richmond Palace for King George II, including a pavilion and an observatory. One can only speculate about the bad blood that developed between the sneezes.

Chambers and Brown continued to bump into each other professionally. They both worked at Blenheim for the Duke of Marlborough, and submitted competing plans for a house for Lord Midleton at Peper Harow. (Lord Midleton didn't like either plan.) In 1769 Brown, though entirely self-taught as an architect of buildings, was chosen by Lord Clive of India to build a new house for him at Claremont, near Esher, a large and important commission. Chambers had already designed two country houses for Clive, and it must have been particularly galling to see this big job go instead to the amateur Brown.

So the professional architect decided to attack the professional gardener on his own ground. It is unclear whether pure jealousy motivated him, or a real conviction that it was time for a fresh approach, but there is no doubt that *A Dissertation on Oriental Gardening* caused a tremendous stir among a bemused – and amused – public. A swingeing personal libel of Brown ('Peasants emerge from the melon grounds to commence professors'), the pamphlet was even more sensational as an over-the-top prospectus for a radically different kind of landscape design, one that promised to be a good deal more fun than the pompous expanses of 'Capability'.

Fifteen years before, Chambers had been fairly straightforward in describing Chinese gardening practices. This time he pulled out all the stops. While it was true, he said, that Chinese garden designers 'have nature for their general model' (just like Brown), they were ready to go very far indeed to make things more exciting. This could mean a variety of pagodas, pavilions and teahouses; artificial rockeries; conservatories and aviaries; even 'Halls of the Moon of a prodigious size . . . pierced with an infinite number of little windows, made to represent the moon and the stars'. It might also mean gardens deliberately planted to create seasonal scenes – a winter forest of evergreens, with glasshouses 'disposed in the form of temples', for example, or a summer plantation with 'a large tract of ground set aside for more secret and voluptuous enjoyments', filled with birds, rare animals and 'all sorts of fragrant and gaudy' flowers, and hidden pavilions staffed with concubines.

This must have brought a shiver of excitement to Chambers's English readers, but what really touched off comment was his claim that Chinese gardeners, 'always on the stretch in search of novelty', did not confine themselves to creating pleasing scenes. They were equally ready to frighten or startle. More so, as Chambers described it.

Where an unimaginative English landscape designer would think only of beauty, a Chinese might deliberately engineer a scene designed to inspire terror in the viewer, or to surprise by means of sudden noises, 'shocks of electrical impulse', strange figures of 'dragons, infernal fiends, and other horrid forms', explosions, earthquakes and artificial storms. All this could well take place in 'gloomy woods' filled with blasted and shattered trees, in which bats, vultures and hungry wolves roamed, and inscribed pillars carried 'pathetical descriptions of tragical events'. To add to the effect, Chambers noted, foundries, lime kilns and glassworks might be concealed on the summits of neighbouring mountains, sending out smoke and flame like volcanoes 'to add to the horror and sublimity of these scenes'.

More soberly – and plausibly – Chambers went on to describe other Chinese gardening practices: the care taken in planting flowers (only the finest forms, arranged so as to avoid sudden transitions in size and colour); the use of potted plants for seasonal succession; the taste for bridges and water pavilions; the absence of lawns and hedges; the constant attention to scale and human interest. Unless you were 'Capability' Brown, it all made sense.

Unfortunately, what the public remembered were the fake volcanoes and the gibbets by the garden paths, and poor Chambers's rocket backfired. Many people took Brown's side. Chambers was forced to produce a revised version of his *Dissertation* arguing that he hadn't meant to criticize Brown alone ('yon stately gentleman in the black perriwig') but all the practitioners of the English landscape style. No sooner had this appeared than William Mason published a clever satirical attack called *An*

Heroic Epistle to Sir William Chambers, which quickly went into fourteen editions. Chambers hadn't a hope. Ironically, he may not even have intended his descriptions of Chinese gardens to be taken literally; employing a hypothetical oriental to comment on European matters was a familiar dodge among writers from Montesquieu to Goldsmith. Chambers's problem was that, as he was an actual expert on things Chinese, readers believed him.

For all the guffaws, the *Dissertation* caught on. On the Continent, where French and German translations reached bestseller status, attempts were even made to realize its more exotic suggestions. In Woerlitz in Germany, Prince Leopold von Anhalt put a working volcano – the Vulkankrater – into his landscape garden. Small Chinese gardens (often called *Anglo-Chinois*) and pavilions cropped up all over France and Belgium, including one built, in an excess of romantic enthusiasm, on top of the ruins of an ancient Roman wall. And in England, the unchallenged reign of 'Capability' Brown, while hardly ended, had at least been shown to be vulnerable to criticism. The *Dissertation* touched a nerve. Years later Humphry Repton, Brown's successor in the grand tradition of large-scale landscaping, was still fussing about Chambers's 'puerile conceits', and unnecessarily pointing out that for his suburban clients, 'scenes of horror, well-calculated for the residence of banditti . . . would be absurd, incongruous and out of character'.

In fairness, it has to be said that Chambers had not been writing about *Chinese* gardening so much as about how *English* gardens could be – and should be – more interesting, more filled with excitement and beauty and things capable of stimulating human feelings. Brown, whose genius was of another order entirely, was perhaps not the most suitable target for the *Dissertation*'s blast. What he created has its own timeless value. But in the hands of less skilled practitioners, working on less appropriate sites, the Brownian groves and endless grass had indeed been in serious danger of becoming a cliché. Chambers at least reminded people there was more to gardening than that.

But was he to be believed about the terrible gardens of China? In an 'Explanatory Discourse' prefacing the second edition of *Observations*, he claimed to have gotten all his information from an impeccable source, an almost certainly imaginary Chinese sculptor named Tan Chetqua, then temporarily resident in London. Privately, Chambers admitted that the trees and plants mentioned had never 'appeared on Chinese paper'. As for the more spectacular items, like the wolves and the volcanoes, well, did it matter? 'For the end of all that I have said,' he wrote, 'was rather as an Artist, to set before you a new style of Gardening; than as a Traveller, to relate what I have really seen.'

The Blue Poppy

I've always been enchanted by the idea of plant hunting. How wonderful to be ploughing through a rhododendron thicket somewhere on the edge of Tibet and come upon some spectacular object that nobody ever knew existed – a black rose, for instance, or maybe an anemone 8 feet tall. The excitement level would be right up there with Howard Carter peering for the very first time into the tomb of King Tutankhamen. The adventures of Robert Fortune (*Rhododendron fortunei*), Reginald Farrer (*Gentiana farreri*), and E. H. 'Chinese' Wilson (*Berberis wilsoniae*) continue to hold much of the fascination of a first-rate detective story for me, accompanied by a certain amount of envy. 'There remain regions of huge promise on the borders of Tibet,' according to Hugh Johnson, and my chances of getting there are slimmer by the year.

Actually, I did get there once. Some thirty years or so ago, when I was a practising journalist, I found myself clinging to some ammunition crates in the back of an Indian Army ton-and-a-half truck as it swayed north to the Tibetan frontier over an appalling and precipitous dirt road. This was plant-hunter country indeed – virtually unexplored rhododendron jungle-cum-rain forest up to 8,000 or 9,000 feet, scrub and rocky, fog-bound Himalayan screes the rest of the way to the 14,500-foot

Se La Pass. Looking back, I can see that I should have snatched the opportunity to elope with a collecting bag. Who knows what I might have found? In point of fact, however, I was prostrate with a combination of altitude and motion sickness, and the only plant that could conceivably have interested me that day was something suicidal – say, hemlock.

Oddly, at the very moment we were bumping toward Tibet, I had with me (though not for plant-hunting purposes) a book by Lieutenant Colonel Frederick Bailey, the man famous for having discovered something approximating a botanical grail: the great blue poppy of Tibet, *Meconopsis betonicifolia*.

In 1913, together with Captain H. T. Morshead, Bailey had made a hair-raising journey along the Tibetan frontier, mapping the route as he went. About thirty years later he got around to writing a book about it. When I was there in 1962 the Chinese (who had occupied Tibet) were threatening to invade India, and the Indian government had banned the sale of maps on security grounds. But Bailey had included maps of the Tibetan border area in his book, and nobody had produced better ones since 1913. That's why I was carrying the book. Once my head and my stomach settled down, the maps proved very useful.

The fact is that Bailey was not a plant hunter at all, but an explorer with a sideline in natural history. While he really cared about answering geographical questions, he was also prepared to identify the habitat of the eared pheasant or to supply the specialists at Kew with pressed samples of a new kind of aconite. Bailey looked like your typical Hyde Park toff, but was actually one of that wonderful English breed of educated hard men who served the Empire and science at the same time. He spoke Tibetan and was prepared to put up with the most difficult conditions of travel, a necessity in country where the passes could be more than 2 miles high and the lower regions rain-drenched and alive with snakes and leeches. His aim on this journey was to penetrate the huge, near-vertical gorges through which Tibet's largest river, the Tsangpo, flowed around the eastern end of the Himalayas into India. These gorges were rumoured to contain waterfalls the size of Niagara. Yet no one had ever managed to see them or even establish that they existed.

It was when Bailey and Morshead were travelling along the Rong River in south-eastern Tibet one day that they came upon 'some grassy meadows covered with alpine flowers' near a place called Lunang. The altitude was over 11,000 feet. Bailey confesses, with mild embarrassment, that he felt no particular excitement at the sight of the tall plants with clear blue blossoms; in fact, the discovery almost passed him by. His diary entry for 10 July 1913 reads, with a bald lack of excitement: 'Among the flowers were blue poppies I had not seen before and purple iris and primulas. There was also a good deal of aconite.' In the report he later prepared for the Indian government, he never even thought to mention the blue poppy.

But it was destined to become famous. A number of meconopses had already been observed growing in this high country on the borders of China, Tibet and India. The intrepid French missionary J. M. Delavay, botanizing a couple of hundred miles east in the Chinese province of Yunnan (shortly before coming down with bubonic plague), had collected a variety of specimens, which he sent back to Paris as mounted samples. One of these, found at an altitude of about 10,000 feet in a sheltered wood near Ho-ching, was given the name *M. betonicifolia* (meaning 'with leaves shaped like betony' – *Stachys officinalis*) when its description was published in Paris in 1889. But Delavay had not managed to gather seed. Bailey didn't either, but he did make careful note of just where he had found the specimens, and also that they were more beautiful than any other poppies he had seen in Tibet. His care would have consequences.

The solution to the mystery of the Tsangpo Gorges eluded Bailey – the last unexplored stretch of the river, some 50 miles, proved impenetrable. But his pressed specimens of the great blue poppy got back to England, where they caused a bit of a stir. They were in bad shape; he had picked only one or two plants, and they were so battered that no one thought of comparing them with Père Delavay's. In Bailey's honour, they were given his name – *M. baileyi*. And by the sound of them – 4 or 5 feet tall, crowned by spectacular blossoms consisting of four large, silky, sky-blue petals unfurling around a heart of golden anthers – they were really something worth having in one's garden.

In 1924, a professional plant collector took to the field. Frank Kingdon-Ward had already made several collecting expeditions on behalf of Kew, commercial seedsmen and private gardeners (including the Dalai Lama himself). This time, he too proposed solving the riddle of the Tsangpo waterfalls. Of course, he would also collect plants and seeds – that was his business. On the way upcountry he stopped in Sikkim to visit Bailey, who was now serving there as British Political Agent, and received from him 'valuable information and advice' about the route into the gorges. They no doubt also talked about the blue poppy, and where to find it.

In mid-June 1924, having crossed into Tibet ('all dust and ice and a raving wind'), Kingdon-Ward came upon his quarry, in the same place Bailey had spotted it. *M. baileyi* – what Kingdon-Ward called 'the woodland blue poppy' – was growing, he reported, 'modestly under the bushes, along the banks of the stream . . . in clumps, half a dozen leafy stems rising from the perennial rootstock to a height of four feet. The flowers flutter out from amongst the sea-green leaves like blue-and-gold butter-flies; each is borne singly on a pedicel, the plant carrying half a dozen nodding, incredibly blue four-petalled flowers, with a wad of golden anthers in the centre.' Best of all, he went on, 'never have I seen a blue poppy which held out such hopes of being hardy, and of easy cultivation in Britain . . .'

In October, Kingdon-Ward dutifully returned to the riverbank to gather seeds. From his description of the process in other places, we may assume that it was hard, unpleasant work. Choice plants had been marked with bits of coloured wool in the summer to make identification easier, but snow often lay across the meadows that had been bright with flowers only a few months before, making it necessary to dig for the ripened seed capsules. Once seeds were harvested, they had to be dried carefully – not always a simple matter when rain and mists, if not snow, were continuous – and in some cases the seeds had to be sorted from the desiccated grubs that also inhabited the capsules. Then came the packing: in envelopes, well wrapped in paper, and placed in biscuit tins that were soldered shut. Some of the best species went back home in thermos flasks to minimize temperature change. One complicated packing experiment, involving sealed containers full of carbon dioxide injected from seltzer cartridges, turned out to be no improvement over plain air.

Kingdon-Ward's blue poppy seeds arrived in England in the spring of 1925 and were promptly distributed to fifty gardens around the country for trial. Seventy-five per cent germinated successfully, causing a sensation. Prize medals flowed in; everybody wanted to grow *M. baileyi*. At the Chelsea Flower Show in 1927, seedling blue poppies went for a guinea apiece. One C. E. Baines ('author of *The Down Train*, etc.') published a 'shocker' called *The Blue Poppy*. In his magisterial *An Account of the Genus Meconopsis*, Sir George Taylor remarked that 'it is given to few plants to attain such popularity so rapidly and to establish themselves so firmly in the estimation of horticulturists'.

Unfortunately for Lieutenant Colonel Bailey, Sir George also made a magisterial decision about the name. *M. baileyi* was clearly the same plant as Père Delavay's *M. betonicifolia* ('that the two plants are conspecific seems evident'). Since *M. betonicifolia* was reported first, we had to forget about *M. baileyi*, which – except for a few stubborn seed catalogues – is the situation that obtains now.

Do many people grow the blue poppy today? I've been tempted to try. I note that you can buy a packet of seed from Sutton's for £1.15, which is certainly cheaper than a trip to Tibet. Sutton's tells me there is no shortage of takers; it puts up about 4,000 packets a year (as against only 700 for the Welsh poppy *M. cambrica*), and sells them mostly by mail order. But it admits that the plant is a little tricky to raise, and a quick survey of gardening books confirms this. Though technically a perennial, in drier gardens it is monocarpic, meaning that it exhausts itself producing seeds and, after flowering once, dies; under those conditions it also may display 'a less acceptable blue'. Everybody agrees that it requires well-drained acid soil in partial shade, and there is no disputing that it has a very short period of bloom. Sir George notes that you can fool a blue poppy into becoming polycarpic if you can discourage it from flowering the first year, in which case it sends up more stalks and behaves the way it was found behaving in Tibet. This sounds sensible. If I were only slightly more ambitious, I'd give it a whack.

I've often wondered if Colonel Bailey ever tried growing his blue poppy. He was supposed to have been an enthusiastic gardener – Kingdon-Ward made a point of noting this when he visited him in Sikkim. But his later adventures were anything but botanical. The most spectacular of them involved sneaking over the Russian border into Tashkent in 1918, after the revolution, as a British secret agent. He actually lived there for six months in disguise, hauling around an all-too-obvious camera, taking pictures and gathering intelligence. When he was in his eighties, living in well-earned retirement in Norfolk, I got into correspondence with him about his pictures, and used some of them in a magazine article. He died soon after. I deeply regret that I never had a chance to meet him, and talk about plant hunting and the Tsangpo Gorges. As Kingdon-Ward discovered after gathering those seeds, incidentally, there were no spectacular waterfalls, only a rather disappointing series of cascades.

Lost Gardens

I've had experience trying to deal with a lost garden. Almost lost, anyway. When we bought our cottage on the edge of Wales it was possible to see – faintly – that someone had once devoted a lot of time and thought and probably love to the gardens surrounding it. For the last thirty years or so, however, nobody had cared. When we arrived, the grass was hay, the beds were mostly bindweed, the hedges small forests, the lilacs toppling, the mahonias monstrous. Cedars threatened to engulf the house. The view – a spectacular one, I now know – lurked unseen behind man-high blackberry brambles, elders, and hazels. I could go on about the nettles, but I won't.

Still, it was recognizably a garden, the work of a gardener. I found irises and day-lilies and peonies and plenty of primroses. There was a flowering quince still struggling to produce the odd deep-pink blossom 15 feet in the air. A few knotted old rosebushes, splendid and fragrant in bloom, covered with bright-red hips in the winter. Fragments of a sweet-bay hedge. Landscaping, too – stone terraces separated different levels of lawn, and the remains of ornamental fencing suggested that my vanished gardener had made plans and actually carried some of them out. But in the end he (or she) faltered, and nature did not. The growing things grew, the stronger defeating the weaker, when we turned up the garden was well on its way to oblivion.

While I hardly regret having saved it – it is a constant challenge and a delight – the very act of bringing it back to life has a quixotic aspect. The world is full of lost gardens, millennia of them. Think of the Hanging Gardens of Babylon, so thoroughly lost that no one even knows what they looked like, or why they were called 'hanging' (most likely it is because they were roof gardens that cascaded from one level to the next). In his memoirs, Cortez described the gardens of Aztec Mexico City as 'the largest, freshest and most beautiful that were ever seen', but he and his fellow conquistadors destroyed them so completely that, looking back much later, he could only mourn their passing: 'Alas! today, all is overthrown and lost, nothing left standing. No future discoveries will ever be so wonderful.'

I recall visiting Coolbawn, an Irish great house burned in the Troubles sixty years ago, and seeing thigh-thick trunks of ivy crawling out through the broken windows to knit themselves into the rhododendrons. Fuchsias created a mass of foliage literally impenetrable except to birds and small animals. That jungle was once a garden, a grand one, too; now it's a testament to the fertility of Irish rain.

Anyone who has wandered through backcountry New England in lilac time knows about those mysterious stands of purple and white you find in the depths of the forest, often near a tumbledown wall. They bloomed in a farmhouse dooryard before the inhabitants gave up their fields and gardens for Ohio or the California gold rush or the Civil War lilac-generations ago. In the abandoned garden the annuals were the first to vanish (except for self-seeders like pot marigolds or foxgloves); then the less aggressive perennials (primroses, say), and last of all the plants that were nearly wild to begin with, like tawny day-lilies, certain low pinks and hollyhocks. Nothing stopped the lilacs, of course, not the scrub elder or maple sprouts. The house descended into compost probably before the last daffodil gave up, but the lilacs will be with us as long as the woods are.

When I first moved to London I worked in an office overlooking the cobblestones of Covent Garden. That used to be *Convent* Garden until some three centuries ago, and old prints show it lined with rows of vegetables and fruit trees bearing lavishly for the monks of Westminster Abbey. In time Covent Garden ceased to grow things to eat and turned to selling them. Even the produce dealers are gone now (it's tough finding a turnip or a head of lettuce among the boutiques), but I don't doubt that there is the odd spading fork rusting quietly away under the pavement, abandoned on a hot summer's day some time in the fourteenth century by a very tired novice. I like to think so, anyway – there's not much green in the Garden these days, unless you count the Moroccan leather in the tourist shops.

I'm not sure why the idea of lost gardens has such poignance, given that every garden is at the mercy of time. Winter itself is a kind of death, no matter how assiduous the gardener may be, and longer periods are bound to bring more profound changes. The most devoted labour can't keep trees from growing, ground cover from spreading, grass from infiltrating gravel paths. But most of us are able to accept – and, with a certain expenditure of energy, contend with – mere botanical exuberance. It's obliteration that shakes you.

Surely one of the sadder experiences that can befall any gardener is to witness the demise of his or her own garden. Walter Stonehouse, a seventeenth-century English clergyman, self-described as 'the worst of poets' (but a fine plantsman), established a famous garden at Darfield in Yorkshire. He grew no fewer than 866 different plants, many of them from the New

World. But he had the bad luck to be on the wrong side in the Civil War. In 1648 Cromwell's commissioners ejected him from Darfield and tossed him into jail. Years later, after the Restoration, he returned to his garden, surveyed the desolation, and despondently added a note in Latin to his proud plant list:

> Alas, but few are here today
> And I have no hope of founding a new colony.

Ironically it is the informal 'cottage' style of garden that seems most vulnerable to the ravages of time. Where subtle shadows and crop marks on an aerial photograph will reveal the formal plan of an Elizabethan garden 400 years old, a cottage garden dependent solely on the natural character and beauty of the plants themselves may be irrecoverable after only a few years' neglect. Plants die; species may become extinct unless someone looks after them. Experts trying to reconstruct some of Gertrude Jekyll's borders from old photographs were stymied when they found many of the plants she used simply unavailable. In seventy years fashions in flowers had changed. Still, with clubs and dealers devoted to preserving old varieties, we are better off in this respect than John Parkinson (author of the punningly titled *Paradisi in Sole Paradisus Terrestris* – 'Park-in-Sun's Terrestrial Paradise'). When he was an old man in the 1650s, he could only dream about the plants he had known in his boyhood and hope that they might still be blooming in some remote, decayed garden.

In Britain, the natural tendency of gardens to vanish has given rise in recent years to a whole new species of historian determined to recover – at least on paper – an accurate sense of the glories devised by such landscape manipulators as 'Capability' Brown and Humphry Repton. (Their lapses, too. One scholar happily notes how Brown, unable to figure out

a way of planting some awkward crags for a Scottish
suggested they be painted green!) Ancient plant lists, pair.
charts and maps, letters and tattered invoices, archaeolog
shovelwork – all these contribute bits of information about ga
dens that now lie beneath golfcourses, fields of sugar beets or
terraced houses in a suburb. There is a society of garden historians that publishes a learned and excellent journal, and at least
one book in which a wide variety of ditches and bumps are
shown to have been landscaping, not Roman fortifications or
Pictish burials.

Yet while the antiquarian in me approves of this historical
research (it *is* fascinating), I'm not at all sure such activity does
justice to the romance of the subject. Better perhaps the sort of
affecting lessons in mortality favoured by classical Chinese poets
like Li Po. 'Who will not remember long-ago gardens?' he
mused, on hearing a flute on a spring night in the T'ang dynasty
capital of Loyang. Or Alexander Pope's stoic acceptance of the
fact that gardens die, even his jewel-like creation at
Twickenham:

> Another age shall see the golden Ear
> Imbrown the slope, and nod on the parterre,
> Deep Harvests bury all his pride had plann'd
> And laughing Ceres reassume the land.

Or, if you prefer, attempts to restore in imagination the reality of a garden that is utterly and completely gone, like John
Tradescant's great garden in London.

There were, in fact, two John Tradescants, father and son,
and both were among the finest horticulturists of their time. The
elder designed and planted gardens for, among others, the Duke
of Buckingham, Lord Salisbury and Henrietta Maria, wife of
the doomed King Charles I. About 1629, being by then fairly

ous, he decided to build his own garden in south
eth, just across the Thames from Westminster in an area
was then mainly fields and orchards.

Tradescant was more than just a good man with a hoe; he was
a fanatical collector – rare plants, unusual trees, stones, birds,
'anything', as he once put it, 'that is strang'. He brought rarities
back from his own travels, and regularly requested friends and
acquaintances, explorers and merchants, to do the same. His
connections were exceptionally good. In the end his gardens
covered several acres and boasted dozens of flowers and trees
that no one had ever grown in England before: cistuses, an
achillea, the American agave, teucreums, *Rudbeckia laciniata*, the
oleaster, the oriental plane tree and many more – even poison
ivy! (Luckily the latter did not thrive in England.) When he died
in 1638 his son John carried on, working for the Queen and
adding many more 'strang' things to the garden and to the
family's private museum, the ragbag of oddities known as
'Tradescant's Ark'. Students and interested citizens frequently
crossed the Thames for a day of botanizing and gawping at the
treasures of the Ark (which included, among other things, poi-
soned daggers and a complete elephant's head), while Tradescant increased the fame of his garden by publishing a detailed
catalogue of its contents. All this proved irresistible to one Elias
Ashmole, an astrologer and fellow collector. On the death of the
younger John Tradescant he managed to get his hands on the
whole establishment, garden, Ark and all.

Ashmole was apparently a somewhat slippery character; in
the course of his taking over the place, Tradescant's widow
mysteriously died by drowning in the garden pond. In any case,
he was a better collector than gardener. The Ark went to
Oxford, to become the basis of the Ashmolean Museum, while
the garden went the way of all neglected gardens. About 1692,

some fifty years later, John Aubrey reported that most of the
rare plants had disappeared, except for 'a very fair Horse-
chesse-nut tree, Some Pine-trees, and Sumach-trees, Phylerees
(*Phyllerea augustifolia*), &c.' The gate, consisting of two large
whalebones, was still there. In 1749 William Watson paid the
garden a visit, finding it 'totally neglected . . . and quite cover'd
by weeds'. But it was not entirely gone: surviving were two
strawberry trees (*Arbutus unedo*), 'the largest I have seen', and a
buckthorn (*Rhamnus cathartica*) with a trunk a foot through, as
well as Solomon's seal, birthwort (*Aristolochia clematitis*) and
(appropriately) ever-living borage (*Pentaglottis sempervivens*).
Not much to make a show, perhaps, but by then the garden had
been abandoned for more than a century. In 1851 another botanist went poking through the weeds without finding anything that
could be traced to the Tradescants. South Lambeth was getting
busier and considerably more built up. Nemesis arrived in 1880,
when the site of the garden, touted as the biggest piece of empty
land within 3 miles of Charing Cross, was sold to developers,
whereupon it promptly disappeared under roughly seventy-five
terraced houses, each with its tiny London garden.

I bicycle down South Lambeth Road every morning on the
way to work. As I pass Tradescant Road, the U-shaped street
that occupies the greater part of the garden tract, South Lambeth Road narrows, the bus fumes grow thicker, and there is
nothing agreeable in view, only the standardized late-Victorian
façades of the dreary little houses that took the place of the
huge American cypresses, the banks of Tradescant's spider-
worts, the strawberry trees and the arbours heavy with vines. I
imagine the sun shining in south Lambeth, the hum of the bees,
and the fragrances of lavenders, jasmines, roses, stocks, olean-
ders. Forty-eight varieties of apples, nearly as many of pears
(including such seductive kinds as Nutmeg Pere and Poyer Irish

Madam), a lemon tree, an orange tree, cherries galore and peaches. All are vanished now.

Not far away, a quarter of a mile or so, in a churchyard adjoining the ancient palace of Lambeth, the London residence of the Archbishop of Canterbury, the Tradescant Trust has established a small garden giving a faint impression of what was lost. It is planted exclusively with varieties listed by John Tradescant the younger in his garden catalogue of 1656. The garden is necessarily modest – no lemon trees, no swamp cypresses – but there are herbs and bees and the warmth of the sun reflected from the mellow walls of St Mary's Church, which contains an engaging little museum of garden history. One can indeed 'remember long-ago gardens'.